DEPARTMENT OF THE TREASURY TECHNICAL EXPLANATION OF THE
CONVENTION BETWEEN THE UNITED STATES OF AMERICA AND THE REPUBLIC
OF POLAND FOR THE AVOIDANCE OF DOUBLE TAXATION AND THE PREVENTION
OF FISCAL EVASION WITH RESPECT TO TAXES ON INCOME

DEPARTMENT OF THE TREASURY TECHNICAL EXPLANATION OF THE CONVENTION BETWEEN THE UNITED STATES OF AMERICA AND THE REPUBLIC OF POLAND FOR THE AVOIDANCE OF DOUBLE TAXATION AND THE PREVENTION OF FISCAL EVASION WITH RESPECT TO TAXES ON INCOME

This is a Technical Explanation of the Convention between the United States and the Republic of Poland for the Avoidance of Double Taxation and the Prevention of Fiscal Evasion with Respect to Taxes on Income, signed at Warsaw on February 13, 2013 (the "Convention").

Negotiations took into account the U.S. Treasury Department's current tax treaty policy, and the Treasury Department's Model Income Tax Convention, published on November 15, 2006 (the "U.S. Model"). Negotiations also took into account the Model Tax Convention on Income and on Capital, published by the Organisation for Economic Cooperation and Development (the "OECD Model"), and recent tax treaties concluded by the United States and Poland.

The Technical Explanation is an official guide to the Convention. It reflects the policies behind particular Convention provisions, as well as understandings reached during the negotiations with respect to the application and interpretation of the Convention. References in the Technical Explanation to "he" or "his" should be read to mean "he or she" or "his or her," respectively. References to the "Code" are to the Internal Revenue Code of 1986, as amended. References to a "Treas. Reg." are to regulations issued under the Code by the Internal Revenue Service and the Treasury Department.

## ARTICLE 1 (GENERAL SCOPE)

*Paragraph 1*

Paragraph 1 of Article 1 provides that the Convention applies only to residents of one or both Contracting States except where the terms of the Convention provide otherwise. Under Article 4 (Resident) a person is generally treated as a resident of a Contracting State if that person is, under the laws of that State, liable to tax therein by reason of domicile, citizenship, residence, or any other criterion of a similar nature. However, if a person is considered a resident of both Contracting States, Article 4 provides rules for determining a single Contracting State of residence (or no Contracting State of residence). This determination governs for all purposes of the Convention.

Certain provisions are applicable to persons who may not be residents of either Contracting State. For example, paragraph 1 of Article 24 (Non-Discrimination) applies to nationals of the Contracting States. In addition, under Article 26 (Exchange of Information), information may be exchanged with respect to residents of third states.

*Paragraph 2*

Paragraph 2 states the generally accepted relationship both between the Convention and domestic law and between the Convention and other agreements between the Contracting States. That is, no provision in the Convention may restrict any exclusion, exemption, deduction, credit or other benefit accorded by the laws of either Contracting State, or by any other agreement to which both Contracting States are parties. The relationship between the non-discrimination provisions of the Convention and the General Agreement on Trade in Services (the "GATS") is addressed in paragraph 3.

Under paragraph 2, for example, if a deduction would be allowed under the Code in computing the U.S. taxable income of a resident of Poland, the deduction also is allowed to that person in computing taxable income under the Convention. Paragraph 2 also means that the Convention may not increase the tax burden on a resident of a Contracting State beyond the burden determined under domestic law. Thus, a right to tax given by the Convention cannot be exercised unless that right also exists under domestic law.

It follows that, under the principle of paragraph 2, a taxpayer's U.S. tax liability need not be determined under the Convention if the Code would produce a more favorable result. A taxpayer may not, however, choose among the provisions of the Code and the Convention in an inconsistent manner in order to minimize tax. Thus, a taxpayer may use the Convention to reduce its taxable income, but may not combine both treaty and Code rules where doing so would be inconsistent with the intent of either set of rules. For example, assume that a resident of Poland has three separate businesses in the United States. One activity is a profitable permanent establishment and the other two are trades or businesses that would earn taxable income under the Code but do not meet the permanent establishment threshold tests of the Convention. One is profitable and the other incurs a loss. Under the Convention, the income of the permanent establishment is taxable in the United States, and both the profit and loss of the other two businesses are ignored. Under the Code, all three would be subject to tax, but the loss would offset the profits of the two profitable ventures. The taxpayer may not invoke the Convention to exclude the profits of the profitable trade or business and invoke the Code to claim the loss of the loss trade or business against the profit of the permanent establishment. (*See* Rev. Rul. 84-17, 1984-1 C.B. 308.) If, however, the taxpayer invokes the Code for the taxation of all three ventures, he would not be precluded from invoking the Convention with respect, for example, to any dividend income he may receive from the United States that is not effectively connected with any of his business activities in the United States.

Similarly, except as provided in paragraph 3, nothing in the Convention can be used to deny any benefit granted by any other agreement to which both Contracting State are parties. For example, if certain benefits are provided for military personnel or military contractors under a Status of Forces Agreement between the United States and Poland, those benefits or protections will be available to residents of the Contracting States regardless of any provisions to the contrary (or silence) in the Convention.

*Paragraph 3*

Paragraph 3 relates to non-discrimination obligations of the Contracting States under the GATS. The provisions of paragraph 3 are an exception to the rule provided in paragraph 2 of this Article under which the Convention shall not restrict in any manner any benefit now or hereafter accorded by any other agreement between the Contracting States.

Subparagraph 3(a) provides that, unless the competent authorities determine that a taxation measure is not within the scope of the Convention, the national treatment obligations of the GATS shall not apply with respect to that measure. Further, any question arising as to the interpretation or application of the Convention, including in particular whether a measure is within the scope of the Convention, shall be considered only by the competent authorities of the Contracting States, and the procedures under the Convention exclusively shall apply to the dispute. Thus, paragraph 3 of Article XXII (Consultation) of the GATS may not be used to bring a dispute before the World Trade Organization unless the competent authorities of both Contracting States have determined that the relevant taxation measure is not within the scope of Article 24 (Non-Discrimination) of the Convention.

The term "measure" for these purposes is defined broadly in subparagraph 3(b). It would include a law, regulation, rule, procedure, decision, administrative action or any other similar provision or action.

*Paragraph 4*

Paragraph 4 contains the traditional saving clause found in all U.S. income tax treaties. The Contracting States reserve their rights, except as provided in paragraph 5, to tax their residents and citizens as provided under their domestic laws, notwithstanding any provisions of the Convention to the contrary. For example, if a resident of Poland performs professional services in the United States and the income from the services is not attributable to a permanent establishment in the United States, Article 7 (Business Profits) would by its terms prevent the United States from taxing the income. If, however, the resident of Poland is also a citizen of the United States, the saving clause permits the United States to include the remuneration in the worldwide income of the citizen and subject it to tax under the normal Code rules (*i.e.*, without regard to Code section 894(a)). Subparagraph 5(a) of Article 1 also preserves the benefits of special foreign tax credit rules applicable to the U.S. taxation of certain U.S. income of its citizens resident in the other Contracting State. *See* paragraph 4 of Article 23 (Relief from Double Taxation).

For purposes of the saving clause, "residence" is determined under Article 4 (Resident). Thus, an individual who is a resident of the United States under the Code (but not a U.S. citizen) but who is determined to be a resident of the Poland under the tie-breaker rules of Article 4 would be subject to U.S. tax only to the extent permitted by the Convention. The United States would not be permitted to apply its domestic law to that person to the extent that its law is inconsistent with the Convention.

However, the person would still be treated as a U.S. resident for U.S. tax purposes other than determining the individual's U.S. tax liability. For example, in determining under Code section 957 whether a foreign corporation is a controlled foreign corporation, shares in that corporation held by the individual would be considered to be held by a U.S. resident. As a result, other U.S. citizens or residents might be deemed to be United States shareholders of a controlled foreign corporation subject to current inclusion of subpart F income recognized by the corporation. *See* Treas. Reg. section 301.7701(b)-7(a)(3).

Under paragraph 4, each Contracting State also reserves its right to tax former citizens and former long-term residents in accordance with domestic law for a period of ten years following the loss of such status. Thus, paragraph 4 allows the United States to tax former U.S. citizens and former U.S. long-term residents in accordance with Code section 877. Section 877 generally applies to a former citizen or long-term resident of the United States who relinquishes citizenship or terminates long-term residency before June 17, 2008 if he fails to certify that he has complied with U.S. tax laws during the 5 preceding years, or if either of the following criteria exceed established thresholds: (a) the average annual net income tax of such individual for the period of 5 taxable years ending before the date of the loss of status; or (b) the net worth of such individual as of the date of the loss of status.

The United States defines "long-term resident" as an individual (other than a U.S. citizen) who is a lawful permanent resident of the United States in at least 8 of the prior 15 taxable years. An individual is not treated as a lawful permanent resident of the United States for any taxable year in which the individual is treated as a resident of Poland under this Convention, or as a resident of any country other than the United States under the provisions of any other U.S. tax treaty, and the individual does not waive the benefits of the relevant tax treaty.

*Paragraph 5*

Paragraph 5 sets forth certain exceptions to the saving clause. The referenced provisions are intended to provide benefits to citizens and residents even if such benefits do not exist under domestic law.

Subparagraph 5(a) lists certain provisions of the Convention that are applicable to all citizens and residents of a Contracting State, despite the general saving clause rule of paragraph 4:

(1) Paragraph 2 of Article 9 (Associated Enterprises) grants the right to a correlative adjustment with respect to income tax due on profits reallocated under Article 9.

(2) Paragraphs 2, 3 and 5 of Article 18 (Pensions, Social Security, Annuities, Alimony and Child Support) provide exemptions from source or residence State taxation for certain pension distributions, social security payments, alimony and child support.

(3) Article 23 (Relief from Double Taxation) confirms to citizens and residents of one Contracting State the benefit of a credit for income taxes paid to the other or an exemption for income earned in the other State. In addition, paragraph 5 of Article 23 coordinates the tax systems of the Contracting States to avoid double taxation that could result from the imposition of an exit tax or similar regime on an individual who ceases to be treated as a resident (as determined under paragraph 1 of Article 4 (Resident)) of one Contracting State and becomes a resident of the other Contracting State.

(4) Article 24 (Non-Discrimination) protects residents and nationals of one Contracting State against the adoption of certain discriminatory taxation practices in the other Contracting State.

(5) Article 25 (Mutual Agreement Procedure) confers certain benefits on citizens and residents of the Contracting States in order to reach and implement solutions to disputes between the two Contracting States.

Subparagraph 5(b) provides a different set of exceptions to the saving clause. The benefits referred to are all intended to be granted to temporary residents of a Contracting State (for example, in the case of the United States, holders of non-immigrant visas), but not to citizens or to persons who have acquired permanent residence in that State. If beneficiaries of these provisions travel from one Contracting State to the other, and remain in the other long enough to become residents under its internal law, but do not acquire permanent residence status (*i.e.*, in the U.S. context, they do not become "green card" holders) and are not citizens of that State, the host State will continue to grant these benefits even if they conflict with the statutory rules. The benefits preserved by this paragraph are: the host country exemptions for government service salaries and pensions under Article 19 (Government Service), certain income of visiting students and trainees under Article 20 (Students and Trainees) and the income of diplomatic agents and consular officers and under Article 27 (Members of Diplomatic Missions and Consular Posts).

*Paragraph 6*

Paragraph 6 addresses special issues presented by the payment of items of income, profit or gain to entities that are fiscally transparent, such as partnerships, estates and trusts. Because countries may take different views as to when an entity is fiscally transparent, the risk of both double taxation and double non-taxation is relatively high. The provision, and the corresponding requirements of the substantive rules of the other Articles of the Convention, should be read with two goals in mind. First, the intention of paragraph 6 is to eliminate a number of technical problems that could prevent investors using such entities from claiming treaty benefits, even though such investors would be subject to tax on the income derived through such entities. Second, the provision prevents a resident of a Contracting State from claiming treaty benefits in circumstances where the resident investing in the entity does not take into account the item of income paid to the entity because the entity is not fiscally transparent in its State of residence.

In general, the principles incorporated in this paragraph reflect the regulations under Treas. Reg. section 1.894-1(d). Treas. Reg. 1.894-1(d)(3)(iii) provides that an entity will be fiscally transparent under the laws of an interest holder's jurisdiction with respect to an item of income to the extent that the laws of that jurisdiction require the interest holder resident in that jurisdiction to separately take into account on a current basis the interest holder's respective share of the item of income paid to the entity, whether or not distributed to the interest holder, and the character and source of the item in the hands of the interest holder are determined as if such item were realized directly by the interest holder. Entities falling under this description in the United States include partnerships, corporations that have made a valid election to be taxed under Subchapter S of Chapter 1 of the Code ("S corporations"), common investment trusts under section 584, simple trusts and grantor trusts. This paragraph also applies to payments made to other entities, such as U.S. limited liability companies ("LLCs"), that may be treated as either partnerships or as disregarded as a separate entity for U.S. tax purposes.

Except as otherwise provided under subparagraph 6(b), under subparagraph 6(a), an item of income, profit or gain derived by or through such a fiscally transparent entity will be considered to be derived by a resident of a Contracting State if a resident is treated under the taxation laws of that State as deriving the item of income. For example, if a company that is a resident of Poland pays interest to an entity that is treated as fiscally transparent for U.S. tax purposes, the interest will be considered derived by a resident of the United States, but only to the extent that the taxation laws of the United States treats one or more U.S. residents (whose status as U.S. residents is determined, for this purpose, under U.S. tax law) as deriving the interest for U.S. tax purposes. Where the entity is a partnership, the persons who are, under U.S. tax laws, treated as partners of the entity would normally be the persons whom the U.S. tax laws would treat as deriving the interest income through the partnership. Also, it follows that persons whom the United States treats as partners but who are not U.S. residents for U.S. tax purposes may not claim a benefit under the Convention for the interest paid to the partnership, because such third-country partners are not residents of the United States for purposes of claiming this benefit. If, however, the country in which the third-country partners are treated as resident for tax purposes, as determined under the laws of that country, has an income tax convention with Poland, they may be entitled to claim a benefit under that convention (these results would also follow in the case of an entity that is disregarded as a separate entity under the laws of one jurisdiction but not the other, such as a single-owner entity that is viewed as a branch for U.S. tax purposes and as a corporation for tax purposes under the laws of Poland). In contrast, where the entity is organized under U.S. laws and is classified as a corporation for U.S. tax purposes, interest paid by a company that is a resident of Poland to the U.S. corporation will be considered derived by a resident of the United States since the U.S. corporation is treated under U.S. taxation laws as a resident of the United States and as deriving the income.

Under subparagraph 6(a), the same result would be reached even if the tax laws of Poland would treat the entity differently (*e.g.*, if the entity were not treated as fiscally transparent in Poland in the first example above where the entity is treated as a partnership for U.S. tax purposes). Similarly, the characterization of the entity in a third country is also irrelevant, even if the entity is organized in that third country, although subparagraph 6(b) imposes an additional requirement in the case of entities organized in a third country.

Subparagraph 6(b) imposes an additional requirement in cases of payments through an entity that is organized in a third country. In such cases, if the entity is not treated as fiscally transparent under the laws of the State in which the income, profit or gains arises, and if the entity is eligible in its own right for benefits under a convention for the avoidance of double taxation between the third state and the State in which the income, profit or gain arises with respect to the particular item of income, profit or gain that are more favorable than the benefits provided under the Convention with respect to that item, subparagraph 6(a) shall not have application. For example, assume that USCo, a corporation resident in the United States, is the sole shareholder of FCo, an entity established in Country F. Under the laws of the United States, FCo is treated as fiscally transparent, but under the laws of Poland, FCo is treated as a corporation. FCo receives Poland-source interest which, under the provisions of Article 11 (Interest) of the Convention, would be subject to tax in Poland at a rate of 5 percent. Pursuant to subparagraph 6(a), USCo would be considered as deriving the Poland-source interest. However, subparagraph 6(b) provides that if the tax treaty between Poland and Country F provides a limitation on the rate of interest withholding that is lower than 5 percent, and if FCo would be eligible for such lower rate in its own right on the payment of interest, USCo shall not be deemed as deriving the interest payment. Nevertheless, FCo may claim the more favorable treaty benefits from Poland in its own right under the tax treaty between Poland and Country F.

The principles of paragraph 6 apply to trusts to the extent that they are fiscally transparent in either Contracting State. For example, suppose that X, a resident of Poland, creates a revocable trust in the United States and names persons resident in a third country as the beneficiaries of the trust. If, under the laws of Poland, X is treated as taking the trust's income into account for tax purposes, the trust's income would be regarded as being derived by a resident of Poland. In contrast, since the determination of deriving an item of income, profit or gain is made on an item by item basis, it is possible that, in the case of a U.S. non-grantor trust, the trust itself may be able to claim benefits with respect to certain items of income, such as capital gains, so long as it is a resident liable to tax on such gains, but not with respect to other items of income that are treated as income of the trust's interest holders.

As noted above, paragraph 6 is not an exception to the saving clause of paragraph 4. Accordingly, paragraph 6 does not prevent a Contracting State from taxing an entity that is treated as a resident of that State under its tax law. For example, if a U.S. LLC with members who are residents of Poland elects to be taxed as a corporation for U.S. tax purposes, the United States will tax that LLC on its worldwide income on a net basis, without regard to whether Poland views the LLC as fiscally transparent.

## ARTICLE 2 (TAXES COVERED)

This Article specifies the U.S. taxes and the taxes of Poland to which the Convention applies. With two exceptions, the taxes specified in Article 2 are the covered taxes for all purposes of the Convention. A broader coverage applies for purposes of Articles 24 (Non-Discrimination) and 26 (Exchange of Information). Article 24 applies with respect to all taxes, including those imposed by state and local governments. Article 26 applies with respect to all taxes imposed at the national level.

*Paragraph 1*

Paragraph 1 identifies the category of taxes to which the Convention applies. Paragraph 1 is based on the OECD Model and defines the scope of application of the Convention. The Convention applies to taxes on income, including gains, imposed on behalf of a Contracting State, irrespective of the manner in which they are levied. Except with respect to Article 24 (Non-Discrimination), state and local taxes are not covered by the Convention.

*Paragraph 2*

Paragraph 2 also is based on the OECD Model and provides a definition of taxes on income and on capital gains. The Convention covers taxes on total income or any part of income and includes tax on gains derived from the alienation of property. The Convention does not apply, however, to social security or unemployment taxes, or any other charges where there is a direct connection between the levy and individual benefits. The Convention also does not apply to property taxes, except with respect to Article 24 (Non-Discrimination) or to Article 26 (Exchange of Information) to the extent that such property taxes are imposed at the national level.

*Paragraph 3*

Paragraph 3 lists the taxes in force at the time of signature of the Convention to which the Convention applies.

The existing covered taxes of Poland are identified in subparagraph 3(a) as the personal income tax and the corporate income tax, hereinafter referred to as "Polish tax".

Subparagraph 3(b) provides that the existing U.S. taxes subject to the rules of the Convention are the Federal income taxes imposed by the Code, together with the Federal taxes imposed on the investment income of foreign private foundations (Code sections 4940 through 4948) hereinafter referred to as "United States tax". Social security and unemployment taxes (Code sections 1401, 3101, 3111 and 3301) are specifically excluded from coverage.

*Paragraph 4*

Under paragraph 4, the Convention will apply to any taxes that are identical, or substantially similar, to those enumerated in paragraph 3, and which are imposed in addition to, or in place of, the existing taxes after February 13, 2013, the date of signature of the Convention. The paragraph also provides that the competent authorities of the Contracting States will notify each other of any significant changes to their taxation laws.

## ARTICLE 3 (GENERAL DEFINITIONS)

Article 3 provides general definitions and rules of interpretation applicable throughout the Convention. Certain other terms are defined in other articles of the Convention. For example, the term "resident of a Contracting State" is defined in Article 4 (Resident). The term "permanent establishment" is defined in Article 5 (Permanent Establishment). These definitions apply for all purposes of the Convention. Other terms, such as "dividends," "interest" and "royalties" are defined in specific Articles for purposes of those Articles.

*Paragraph 1*

Paragraph 1 defines a number of basic terms used in the Convention. The introduction to paragraph 1 makes clear that these definitions apply for all purposes of the Convention, unless the context requires otherwise. This latter condition allows flexibility in the interpretation of the Convention in order to avoid results not intended by the Convention's negotiators.

Subparagraph 1(a) defines the term "person" to include an individual, an estate, a trust, a partnership, a company and any other body of persons. The definition is significant for a variety of reasons. For example, under Article 4, only a "person" can be a "resident" and therefore eligible for most benefits under the treaty. Also, all "persons" are eligible to claim relief under Article 25 (Mutual Agreement Procedure).

The term "company" is defined in subparagraph 1(b) as a body corporate or an entity treated as a body corporate for tax purposes in the state where it is organized. The definition refers to the law of the state in which an entity is organized in order to ensure that an entity that is treated as fiscally transparent in its country of residence will not get inappropriate benefits, such as the reduced withholding rate provided by subparagraph 2(b) of Article 10 (Dividends). It also ensures that the Limitation on Benefits provisions of Article 22 will be applied at the appropriate level.

The terms "enterprise of a Contracting State" and "enterprise of the other Contracting State" are defined in subparagraph 1(c) as an enterprise carried on by a resident of a Contracting State and an enterprise carried on by a resident of the other Contracting State. An enterprise of a Contracting State need not be carried on in that State. It may be carried on in the other Contracting State or a third state (*e.g.*, a U.S. corporation doing all of its business in Poland would still be a U.S. enterprise).

Subparagraph 1(c) further provides that these terms also encompass an enterprise conducted through an entity (such as a partnership) that is treated as fiscally transparent in the Contracting State where the entity's owner is resident. The definition makes this point explicitly to ensure that the purpose of the Convention is not thwarted by an overly technical application of the term "enterprise of a Contracting State" to activities carried on through partnerships and similar entities. In accordance with Article 4 (Resident), an entity that is fiscally transparent in the Contracting State in which it is organized is not considered to be a resident of that Contracting State (although income derived through such an entity may be taxed as the income of a resident of a Contracting State to the extent that it is taxed in the hands of resident partners or other resident owners). The definition makes clear that as provided in Article 1 (General Scope) paragraph 6, an enterprise conducted by such an entity will be treated as carried on by a resident of a Contracting State to the extent its partners or other owners are residents. This approach is consistent with Code section 875, which attributes a trade or business conducted by a partnership to its partners and a trade or business conducted by an estate or trust to its beneficiaries.

Subparagraph 1(d) defines the term "enterprise" as any activity or set of activities that constitutes the carrying on of a business. The term "business" is not defined, but subparagraph 1(e) provides that it includes the performance of professional services and other activities of an independent character. Both subparagraphs are identical to definitions added to the OECD Model in connection with the deletion of Article 14 (Independent Personal Services) from the OECD Model in 2000. The inclusion of the two definitions is intended to clarify that income from the performance of professional services or other activities of an independent character is dealt with under Article 7 (Business Profits) and not Article 21 (Other Income).

Subparagraph 1(f) defines the term "international traffic." The term means any transport by a ship or aircraft except when such transport is solely between places within a Contracting State. This definition is applicable principally in the context of Article 8 (Shipping and Air Transport). The definition combines with paragraphs 2 and 3 of Article 8 to exempt from tax by the source State: profits from the rental of ships or aircraft on a full (time or voyage) basis; profits from the rental on a bareboat basis of ships or aircraft if the rental income is incidental to profits from the operation of ships or aircraft in international traffic; profits from the rental on a bareboat basis of ships or aircraft if such ships or aircraft are operated in international traffic by the lessee; and profits of an enterprise of a Contracting State from the use, maintenance, or rental of containers (including trailers, barges, and related equipment for the transport of containers), where such use, maintenance or rental, as the case may be, is incidental to the operation of ships or aircraft in international traffic.

The exclusion from international traffic of transport solely between places within a Contracting State means, for example, that carriage of goods or passengers solely between New York and Chicago would not be treated as international traffic, whether carried by a U.S. or a foreign carrier. The substantive taxing rules of the Convention relating to the taxation of income from transport, principally Article 8, therefore, would not apply to income from such carriage. Thus, if the carrier engaged in internal U.S. traffic were a resident of Poland (assuming that were possible under U.S. law), the United States would not be required to exempt the income from that transport under Article 8. The income would, however, be treated as business profits under Article 7 (Business Profits), and therefore would be taxable in the United States only if attributable to a U.S. permanent establishment of the foreign carrier, and then only on a net basis. The gross basis U.S. tax imposed by section 887 would not apply under the circumstances described. If, however, goods or passengers are carried by a carrier resident in Poland from a non-U.S. port to, for example, New York, and some of the goods or passengers continue on to Chicago, the entire transport would be international traffic. This would be true if the international carrier transferred the goods at the U.S. port of entry from a ship to a land vehicle, from a ship to a lighter, or even if the overland portion of the trip in the United States was handled by an independent carrier under contract with the original international carrier, so long as both parts of the trip were reflected in original bills of lading. For this reason, the U.S. Model refers, in the definition of "international traffic," to "such transport" being solely between places in the other Contracting State, while the OECD Model refers to the ship or aircraft being operated solely between such places. The U.S. Model language is intended to make clear that, as in the above example, even if the goods are carried on a different aircraft for the internal portion of the international voyage than is used for the overseas portion of the trip, the definition applies to that internal portion as well as the external portion.

Finally, a "cruise to nowhere," *i.e.*, a cruise beginning and ending in a port in the same Contracting State with no stops in a foreign port, would not constitute international traffic.

Subparagraph 1(g) defines the term "competent authorities" for Poland and the United States. The U.S. competent authority is the Secretary of the Treasury or his delegate. The Secretary of the Treasury has delegated the competent authority function to the Commissioner of Internal Revenue, who in turn has delegated the authority to the Deputy Commissioner

(International) LB&I.  With respect to interpretative issues, the Deputy Commissioner (International) LB&I acts with the concurrence of the Associate Chief Counsel (International) of the Internal Revenue Service.  The competent authority in the case of Poland is the Minister of Finance or his authorized representative.

The geographical scope of the Convention with respect to Poland is set out in subparagraph 1(h).  The term "Poland" means the Republic of Poland, including the territorial sea thereof and any area outside the territorial sea of the Republic of Poland designated under its laws and in accordance with international law as an area within which the sovereign rights of the Republic of Poland with respect to the sea bed and sub-soil and their natural resources may be exercised.

The geographical scope of the Convention with respect to the United States is set out in subparagraph 1(i).  It encompasses the United States of America, including the states, the District of Columbia, and the territorial sea of the United States.  The term does not include Puerto Rico, the United States Virgin Islands, Guam or any other U.S. possession or territory.  For certain purposes, the term "United States" includes the sea bed and subsoil of undersea areas adjacent to the territorial sea of the United States.  This extension applies to the extent that the United States may exercise sovereignty in accordance with international law for the purpose of natural resource exploration and exploitation of such areas.  This extension of the definition applies, however, only if the person, property or activity to which the Convention is being applied is connected with such natural resource exploration or exploitation.  Thus, it would not include any activity involving the sea floor of an area over which the United States exercised sovereignty for natural resource purposes if that activity was unrelated to the exploration and exploitation of natural resources.  This result is consistent with the result that would be obtained under Code section 638, which treats the continental shelf as part of the United States for purposes of natural resource exploration and exploitation.

The term "national," as it relates to the United States and to Poland, is defined in subparagraph 1(j).  This term is relevant for purposes of Article 4 (Resident), Article 19 (Government Service) and Article 24 (Non-Discrimination).  A national of one of the Contracting States is either an individual who is a citizen or national of that State, or any legal person, partnership or association deriving its status, as such, from the law in force in the State where it is established.

Subparagraph 1(k) defines the term "pension fund".  The term means any person that is established in a Contracting State and satisfies two criteria.  First, as provided in clause 1(k)(i), the person must be generally exempt from income taxation in the Contracting State in which it is established.  Second, as provided in clause 1(k)(ii), the person must be operated principally either to administer or provide pension or retirement benefits, or to earn income for the benefit of one or more persons established in the same Contracting State that are generally exempt from income taxation in that Contracting State and are operated principally to administer or provide pension or retirement benefits.

The definition recognizes that pension funds sometimes administer or provide benefits other than pension or retirement benefits, such as death benefits.  However, in order for the fund to be considered a pension fund for purposes of the Convention, the provision of any other such benefits must be merely incidental to the fund's principal activity of administering or providing pension or retirement benefits. The definition also ensures that if a fund is a collective fund that earns income for the benefit of other funds, then substantially all of the funds that participate in the collective fund must be residents of the same Contracting State as the collective fund and must be entitled to benefits under the Convention in their own right.

In the case of the United States, the term "pension fund" includes the following: a trust providing pension or retirement benefits under a Code section 401(a) qualified pension plan (which includes a Code section 401(k) plan); a profit sharing or stock bonus plan; a Code section 403(a) qualified annuity plan; a Code section 403(b) plan; a trust that is an individual retirement account under Code section 408; a Roth individual retirement account under Code section 408A or a simple retirement account under Code section 408(p); a trust providing pension or retirement benefits under a simplified employee pension plan under Code section 408(k); a trust described in section 457(g) providing pension or retirement benefits under a Code section 457(b) plan; and the Thrift Savings Fund (section 7701(j)). A group trust described in Rev. Rul. 81-100, as amended by Rev. Rul. 2004-67 and Rev. Rul. 2011-1, qualifies as a pension fund only if substantially all of its activity is to earn income for the benefit of pension funds that are themselves entitled to benefits under the Convention as a resident of the United States.

*Paragraph 2*

Terms that are not defined in the Convention are dealt with in paragraph 2.

Paragraph 2 provides that in the application of the Convention, any term used but not defined in the Convention will have the meaning that it has under the domestic law of the Contracting State whose tax is being applied, unless the context requires otherwise. If the term is defined under both the tax and non-tax laws of a Contracting State, the definition in the tax law will take precedence over the definition in the non-tax laws. Finally, there also may be cases where the tax laws of a State contain multiple definitions of the same term. In such a case, the definition used for purposes of the particular provision at issue, if any, should be used.

The reference in paragraph 2 to the domestic law of a Contracting State means the law in effect at the time the treaty is being applied, not the law as in effect at the time the treaty was signed. The use of "ambulatory" definitions, however, may lead to results that are at variance with the intentions of the negotiators and of the Contracting States when the treaty was negotiated and ratified. The inclusion in both paragraphs 1 and 2 of an exception to the generally applicable definitions where the "context otherwise requires" is intended to address this circumstance. Where reflecting the intent of the Contracting States requires the use of a definition that is different from a definition under paragraph 1 or the law of the Contracting State applying the Convention, that definition will apply. Thus, flexibility in defining terms is necessary and permitted.

## ARTICLE 4 (RESIDENT)

This Article sets forth rules for determining whether a person is a resident of a

Contracting State for purposes of the Convention. As a general matter, only residents of the Contracting States may claim the benefits of the Convention. The treaty definition of residence is to be used only for purposes of the Convention. The fact that a person is determined to be a resident of a Contracting State under Article 4 does not automatically entitle that person to the benefits of the Convention. In order to obtain the benefits of the Convention, such person must satisfy all applicable requirements specified in the Convention, including other applicable requirements of Article 1 (General Scope), beneficial ownership and Article 22 (Limitation on Benefits).

The determination of residence for treaty purposes looks first to a person's liability to tax as a resident under the respective taxation laws of the Contracting States. As a general matter, a person is liable to tax as a resident under the domestic laws of one Contracting State and not of the other need look no further. For purposes of the Convention, that person is a resident of the State in which he is liable to tax as resident under domestic law. If, however, a person is liable to tax as a resident under the domestic laws of both Contracting States, the Article uses tie-breaker rules to assign a single State of residence (or no State of residence) to such a person for purposes of the Convention.

*Paragraph 1*

The term "resident of a Contracting State" is defined in paragraph 1. In general, this definition incorporates the definitions of residence in U.S. and Polish law by referring to a resident as a person who, under the laws of a Contracting State, is liable to tax therein by reason of his domicile, residence, citizenship, place of management, place of incorporation or any other similar criterion. Thus, residents of the United States include aliens who are considered U.S. residents under Code section 7701(b), entities organized in the United States and that have elected under Treas. Reg. 301.7701-2 to be taxed by the United States as a corporation, and companies that are treated as domestic corporations under Code section 7874(b). Paragraph 1 also specifically includes the two Contracting States, and political subdivisions and local authorities of the two States, as residents for purposes of the Convention.

The fact that a particular entity does not pay tax in practice will not necessarily mean that the entity is not a resident. An entity that is not fiscally transparent in its Contracting State of residence for purposes of paragraph 6 of Article 1 (General Scope), and is not unconditionally exempt from tax, will generally be treated as a resident for purposes of the Convention. This is generally true even for an entity that, in practice, is not required to pay tax if it meets certain requirements with respect to its activities, types of income, or distribution practices. For example, a U.S. Regulated Investment Company (RIC) and a U.S. Real Estate Investment Trust (REIT) are residents of the United States for purposes of the treaty. These entities are taxable to the extent that they do not currently distribute their profits, and therefore may be regarded as liable to tax, even though these entities do not generally have taxable income in practice. They also must satisfy a number of requirements under the Code in order to be entitled to their particular tax treatment.

A person who is liable to tax in a Contracting State only in respect of income from sources within that State or of profits attributable to a permanent establishment in that State will not be treated as a resident of that Contracting State for purposes of the Convention. Thus, a consular official of the other Contracting State who is posted in the United States, who may be subject to U.S. tax on U.S. source investment income, but is not taxable in the United States on non-U.S. source income (*see* Code section 7701(b)(5)(B)), would not be considered a resident of the United States for purposes of the Convention. Similarly, an enterprise of Poland with a permanent establishment in the United States is not, by virtue of that permanent establishment, a resident of the United States. The enterprise generally is subject to U.S. tax only with respect to its income that is attributable to the U.S. permanent establishment, not with respect to its worldwide income, as it would be if it were a U.S. resident.

*Paragraph 2*

Paragraph 2 provides that entities such as pension funds as defined in Article 3 (General Definitions) and legal persons organized under the laws of a Contracting State and established exclusively for religious, charitable, scientific, artistic, cultural, or educational purposes are residents of the Contracting State in which they are established or organized. Such persons are liable to tax, notwithstanding that all or part of its income or gains may be exempt from tax under the domestic laws of that State. Thus, a section 501(c) organization organized in the United States (such as a U.S. charity) that is generally exempt from tax under U.S. law is nevertheless a resident of the United States for all purposes of the Convention.

*Paragraph 3*

If, under the domestic law of both Contracting States, and, thus, under paragraph 1, an individual is a resident of both Contracting States, a series of tie-breaker rules are provided in paragraph 3 to determine a single State of residence for that individual. These tests are to be applied in the order in which they are stated. The first test is based on where the individual has a permanent home. If that test is inconclusive because the individual has a permanent home available to him in both States, he will be considered to be a resident of the Contracting State where his personal and economic relations are closest (i.e., the location of his "center of vital interests"). If that test is also inconclusive, or if he does not have a permanent home available to him in either State, he will be treated as a resident of the Contracting State where he maintains a habitual abode. If he has a habitual abode in both States or in neither of them, he will be treated as a resident of the Contracting State of which he is a national. If he is a national of both States or of neither, the competent authorities shall endeavor to settle the question by mutual agreement.

*Paragraph 4*

Paragraph 4 addresses dual residence issues for companies. A company is treated as resident in the United States if it is created or organized under the laws of the United States or a political subdivision. If, as is frequently the case, a company is treated as a resident of Poland if it is either incorporated or managed and controlled there, dual residence can arise in the case of a U.S. company that is managed and controlled in Poland. In other cases, a company may be a dual resident because it was originally incorporated in one Contracting State but has "continued" into the other Contracting State. Paragraph 4 thus attempts to deal with each of these situations.

Under paragraph 4, the residence of a dual resident company will be in the Contracting State under the laws of which it is created or organized if it is created or organized under the laws of only one of the other Contracting States. Thus, if a company is a resident of the United States because it is incorporated under the laws of one of the states and is a resident of Poland because its place of effective management is in Poland, then it will be a resident only of the United States. However, if the incorporation test does not resolve the question because, for example, the company was incorporated in one Contracting State and continued into the other Contracting State, but the first-mentioned Contracting State does not recognize the migration and continues to treat the company as a resident, the case would then be addressed by paragraph 5.

*Paragraph 5*

Paragraph 5 addresses situations when by reason of the provisions of paragraph 1, 2 or 4, a person other than an individual is a resident of both Contracting States. In such cases, the competent authorities of the Contracting States may, but are not required to, use the mutual agreement procedure to endeavor to determine the mode of application to the dual resident person. If the competent authorities do not reach a mutual agreement regarding a single State of residence, such dual resident person cannot claim any benefit accorded to residents of a Contracting State by the Convention. The person may, however, claim any benefits that are not limited to residents, such as those provided by paragraph 1 of Article 24 (Non-Discrimination). Thus, for example, a State cannot impose discriminatory taxation on a dual resident person.

Regardless of the outcome under this paragraph, dual resident companies may be treated as a resident of a Contracting State for purposes other than that of obtaining benefits under the Convention. For example, if a dual resident company pays a dividend to a resident of Poland, the U.S. paying agent would withhold on that dividend at the appropriate treaty rate (assuming the payee is entitled to treaty benefits), because reduced withholding is a benefit enjoyed by the resident of Poland, not by the dual resident company. The dual resident company that paid the dividend would, for this purpose, be treated as a resident of the United States under the Convention. In addition, information relating to dual resident companies can be exchanged under the Convention because, by its terms, Article 26 (Exchange of Information) is not limited to residents of the Contracting States.

## ARTICLE 5 (PERMANENT ESTABLISHMENT)

This Article defines the term "permanent establishment," a term that is significant for several articles of the Convention. The existence of a permanent establishment in a Contracting State is necessary under Article 7 (Business Profits) for the taxation by that State of the business profits of a resident of the other Contracting State. Articles 10 (Dividends), 11 (Interest) and 13 (Royalties) provide for reduced rates of tax at source on payments of these items of income to a resident of the other State only when the income is not attributable to a permanent establishment that the recipient has in the source State. The concept is also relevant in determining which Contracting State may tax certain gains under Article 14 (Capital Gains) and certain "other income" under Article 21 (Other Income).

*Paragraph 1*

The basic definition of the term "permanent establishment" is contained in paragraph 1. As used in the Convention, the term means a fixed place of business through which the business of an enterprise is wholly or partly carried on. As indicated in the OECD Commentary to Article 5 (*see* paragraphs 4 through 8), a general principle to be observed in determining whether a permanent establishment exists is that the place of business must be "fixed" in the sense that a particular building or physical location is used by the enterprise for the conduct of its business, and that it must be foreseeable that the enterprise's use of this building or other physical location will be more than temporary. If an enterprise carries on a business through a sub-contractor, a permanent establishment may also exist for the enterprise if all the requirements of Article 5 are met. For example, under paragraph 1, a permanent establishment may exist where an enterprise carries on its business through sub-contractors at a fixed place of business of the enterprise. Factors that indicate that a location is a fixed place of business of the enterprise, (i.e., a general contractor) include legal possession of the site, controlling access to and use of the site, and overall responsibility for what happens at the location.

*Paragraph 2*

Paragraph 2 lists a number of types of fixed places of business that constitute a permanent establishment. This list is illustrative and non-exclusive. According to paragraph 2, the term permanent establishment includes a place of management, a branch, an office, a factory, a workshop, and a mine, oil or gas well, quarry or other place of extraction of natural resources.

*Paragraph 3*

This paragraph provides rules to determine whether a building site or a construction, assembly or installation project, or an installation or drilling rig or ship used for the exploration of natural resources constitutes a permanent establishment for the contractor, driller, etc. Such a site or activity does not create a permanent establishment unless the site, project, etc. lasts, or the exploration activity continues, for more than twelve months. It is only necessary to refer to "exploration" and not "exploitation" in this context because exploitation activities are defined to constitute a permanent establishment under subparagraph (f) of paragraph 2. Thus, a drilling rig does not constitute a permanent establishment if a well is drilled in twelve months or less. However, the well becomes a permanent establishment as of the date that production begins.

The twelve-month test applies separately to each site or project. The twelve-month period begins when work (including preparatory work carried on by the enterprise) physically begins in a Contracting State. A series of contracts or projects by a contractor that are interdependent both commercially and geographically are to be treated as a single project for purposes of applying the twelve-month threshold test. For example, the construction of a housing development would be considered as a single project even if each house were constructed for a different purchaser.

In applying this paragraph, time spent by a sub-contractor on a building site is counted as time spent by the general contractor at the site for purposes of determining whether the general contractor has a permanent establishment. However, for the sub-contractor itself to be treated as having a permanent establishment, the sub-contractor's activities at the site must last for more than twelve months. For purposes of applying the twelve-month rule, time is measured from the first day the sub-contractor is on the site until the last day. Thus, if a sub-contractor is on a site intermittently, intervening days that the sub-contractor is not on the site are counted.

These interpretations of the Article are based on the Commentary to paragraph 3 of Article 5 of the OECD Model, which contains language that is substantially the same as that in the Convention. These interpretations are consistent with the generally accepted international interpretation of the relevant language in paragraph 3 of Article 5 of the Convention.

If the twelve-month threshold is exceeded, the site or project constitutes a permanent establishment from the first day of activity.

*Paragraph 4*

This paragraph contains exceptions to the general rule of paragraph 1, listing a number of activities that may be carried on through a fixed place of business but which nevertheless do not create a permanent establishment. The use of facilities solely to store, display or deliver merchandise belonging to an enterprise does not constitute a permanent establishment of that enterprise. The maintenance of a stock of goods belonging to an enterprise solely for the purpose of storage, display or delivery, or solely for the purpose of processing by another enterprise does not give rise to a permanent establishment of the first-mentioned enterprise. The maintenance of a fixed place of business solely for the purpose of purchasing goods or merchandise, or for collecting information, for the enterprise, or for other activities that have a preparatory or auxiliary character for the enterprise, such as advertising, or the supply of information, do not constitute a permanent establishment of the enterprise. Moreover, subparagraph 4(f) provides that a combination of the activities described in the other subparagraphs of paragraph 4 will not give rise to a permanent establishment if the combination results in an overall activity that is of a preparatory or auxiliary character.

*Paragraph 5*

Paragraphs 5 and 6 specify when activities carried on by an agent or other person acting on behalf of an enterprise create a permanent establishment of that enterprise. Under paragraph 5, a person is deemed to create a permanent establishment of the enterprise if that person has and habitually exercises an authority to conclude contracts on behalf of the enterprise. If, however, his activities are limited to those activities specified in paragraph 4 which would not constitute a permanent establishment if carried on by the enterprise through a fixed place of business, the person does not create a permanent establishment of the enterprise.

The reference to the ability to habitually exercising an authority to conclude contracts "on behalf of" an enterprise should be interpreted consistently with the analogous terms found in the OECD Model "in the name of that enterprise" and the U.S. Model "binding on the enterprise." As indicated in paragraph 32 to the OECD Commentaries on Article 5, paragraph 5 of the Article is intended to encompass persons who have "sufficient authority to bind the enterprise's participation in the business activity in the State concerned."

17

*Paragraph 6*

Under paragraph 6, an enterprise is not deemed to have a permanent establishment in a Contracting State merely because it carries on business in that State through an independent agent, including a broker or general commission agent, if the agent is acting in the ordinary course of his business. Thus, there are two conditions that must be satisfied: the agent must be both legally and economically independent of the enterprise; and the agent must be acting in the ordinary course of its business in carrying out activities on behalf of the enterprise.

Whether the agent and the enterprise are independent is a factual determination. Among the questions to be considered is the extent to which the agent operates on the basis of instructions from the enterprise. An agent that is subject to detailed instructions regarding the conduct of its operations or to comprehensive control by the enterprise is not legally independent.

In determining whether the agent is economically independent, a relevant factor is the extent to which the agent bears business risk. Business risk refers primarily to risk of loss. An independent agent typically bears risk of loss from its own activities. In the absence of other factors that would establish dependence, an agent that shares business risk with the enterprise, or has its own business risk, is economically independent because its business activities are not integrated with those of the principal. Conversely, an agent that bears little or no risk from the activities it performs is not economically independent and therefore is not described in paragraph 6.

Another relevant factor in determining whether an agent is economically independent is whether the agent acts exclusively or nearly exclusively for the principal. Such a relationship may indicate that the principal has economic control over the agent. A number of principals acting in concert also may have economic control over an agent. The limited scope of the agent's activities and the agent's dependence on a single source of income may indicate that the agent lacks economic independence. It should be borne in mind, however, that exclusivity is not in itself a conclusive test; an agent may be economically independent notwithstanding an exclusive relationship with the principal if it has the capacity to diversify and acquire other clients without substantial modifications to its current business and without substantial harm to its business profits. Thus, exclusivity should be viewed merely as a pointer to further investigation of the relationship between the principal and the agent. Each case must be addressed on the basis of its own facts and circumstances.

*Paragraph 7*

This paragraph clarifies that a company that is a resident of a Contracting State is not deemed to have a permanent establishment in the other Contracting State merely because it controls, or is controlled by, a company that is a resident of that other Contracting State, or that carries on business in that other Contracting State. The determination of whether a permanent establishment exists is made solely on the basis of the factors described in paragraphs 1 through 6 of the Article. Whether a company is a permanent establishment of a related company, therefore, is based solely on those factors and not on the ownership or control relationship between the companies.

## ARTICLE 6 (INCOME FROM REAL PROPERTY)

*Paragraph 1*

The first paragraph of Article 6 states the general rule that income of a resident of a Contracting State derived from real property situated in the other Contracting State may be taxed in the Contracting State in which the property is situated. The paragraph specifies that income from real property includes income from agriculture and forestry.

This Article does not grant an exclusive taxing right to the situs State; the situs State is merely given the primary right to tax. The Article does not impose any limitation in terms of rate or form of tax on the situs State.

*Paragraph 2*

The term "real property" is defined in paragraph 2 by reference to the domestic law definition in the situs State. In the case of the United States, the term has the meaning given to it by Treas. Reg. 1.897-1(b). In addition to the statutory definitions in the two Contracting States, the paragraph specifies certain additional classes of property that, regardless of domestic law definitions are within the scope of the term for purposes of the Convention. This expanded definition conforms to that in the OECD Model. With respect to the United States, the definition of "real property" for purposes of Article 6 is more limited than the reference to a "United States real property interest" in paragraph 2 of Article 14 (Capital Gains). The Article 14 term includes not only real property as defined in Article 6 but certain other interests in real property.

*Paragraph 3*

Paragraph 3 makes clear that all forms of income derived from the exploitation of real property are taxable in the Contracting State in which the property is situated. This includes income from any use of real property, including, but not limited to, income from direct use by the owner (in which case income may be imputed to the owner for tax purposes) and rental income from the letting of real property. In the case of a net lease of real property, if a net election has not been made, the gross rental payment (before deductible expenses incurred by the lessee) is treated as income from the property.

Other income closely associated with real property is covered by other Articles of the Convention, however, and not Article 6. For example, income from the disposition of an interest in real property is not considered "derived" from real property; taxation of that income is addressed in Article 14. Interest paid on a mortgage on real property would be covered by Article 11 (Interest). Distributions by a U.S. REIT or certain regulated investment companies would fall under Article 14 in the case of distributions of U.S. real property gain or Article 10 (Dividends) in the case of distributions treated as dividends. Finally, distributions from a United States Real Property Holding Corporation as defined under Code section 897(c)(2) are not considered to be income from the exploitation of real property; such payments would fall under Article 10 or Article 14.

*Paragraph 4*

This paragraph specifies that the basic rule of paragraph 1 (as elaborated in paragraph 3) applies to income from real property of an enterprise. This clarifies that the situs country may tax the real property income (including rental income) of a resident of the other Contracting State in the absence of attribution to a permanent establishment in the situs State. This provision represents an exception to the general rule under Articles 7 (Business Profits) that income must be attributable to a permanent establishment in order to be taxable in the situs state.

## ARTICLE 7 (BUSINESS PROFITS)

This Article provides rules for the taxation by a Contracting State of the business profits of an enterprise of the other Contracting State.

*Paragraph 1*

Paragraph 1 states the general rule that business profits of an enterprise of one Contracting State may not be taxed by the other Contracting State unless the enterprise carries on business in that other Contracting State through a permanent establishment (as defined in Article 5 (Permanent Establishment)) situated there. When that condition is met, the State in which the permanent establishment is situated may tax the enterprise on the income that is attributable to the permanent establishment.

Although the Convention does not include a definition of "business profits," the term is intended to cover income derived from any trade or business. In accordance with this broad definition, the term "business profits" includes income attributable to notional principal contracts and other financial instruments to the extent that the income is attributable to a trade or business of dealing in such instruments or is otherwise related to a trade or business (as in the case of a notional principal contract entered into for the purpose of hedging currency risk arising from an active trade or business). Any other income derived from such instruments is, unless specifically covered in another article, dealt with under Article 21 (Other Income).

In addition, as a result of the definitions of "enterprise" and "business" in Article 3 (General Definitions), the term includes income derived from the furnishing of personal services. Thus, a consulting firm resident in one State whose employees or partners perform services in the other State through a permanent establishment may be taxed in that other State on a net basis under Article 7, and not under Article 15 (Income from Employment), which applies only to income of employees. With respect to the enterprise's employees themselves, however, their salary remains subject to Article 15.

Because this Article applies to income earned by an enterprise from the furnishing of personal services, the Article also applies to income derived by a partner resident in a

Contracting State that is attributable to personal services performed in the other Contracting State through a partnership with a permanent establishment in that other State. Income which may be taxed under this Article includes all income attributable to the permanent establishment in respect of the performance of the personal services carried on by the partnership (whether by the partner himself, other partners in the partnership, or by employees assisting the partners) and any income from activities ancillary to the performance of those services (*e.g.*, charges for facsimile services).

The application of Article 7 to a service partnership may be illustrated by the following example: a partnership formed in Poland has five partners (who agree to split profits equally), four of whom are resident and perform personal services only in Poland at Office A, and one of whom is a resident and performs personal services at Office B, a permanent establishment in the United States. In this case, the four partners of the partnership resident in Poland may be taxed in the United States in respect of their share of the income attributable to the permanent establishment, Office B. The services giving rise to income which may be attributed to the permanent establishment would include not only the services performed by the one resident partner, but also, for example, if one of the four other partners came to the United States and worked on an Office B matter there, the income in respect of those services. Income from the services performed by the visiting partner would be subject to tax in the United States regardless of whether the visiting partner actually visited or made use of Office B while performing services in the United States.

*Paragraph 2*

Paragraph 2 provides rules for the attribution of business profits to a permanent establishment under which the attributed business profits are determined as if the permanent establishment were a separate enterprise that is independent from the rest of the enterprise of which it is a part, as well as from any other person. The Contracting States will attribute to a permanent establishment the profits that it would have earned had it been a distinct and separate enterprise engaged in the same or similar activities under the same or similar conditions and dealing wholly independently with the enterprise of which it is a permanent establishment. However, the business profits attributable to a permanent establishment are limited to those profits derived from the functions performed, assets used and risks assumed by the permanent establishment.

Whereas paragraph 2 of Article 7 of the OECD Model provides that the paragraph applies "[F]or the purposes of this Article and Article [23A][23B]," paragraph 2 Article 7 applies only for purposes of attributing business profits, and does not have relevance for purposes of relief from double taxation, other than the narrow circumstances as provided in paragraph 3 of this Article (described below).

The "attributable to" concept of paragraph 2 employs the arm's length principle reflected in the report of the OECD "2010 Report on the Attribution of Profits to Permanent Establishments" (the "2010 Report") for determining the amount of business profits that shall be taxable to a permanent establishment, in place of the analogous principles in Code section 864(c). In effect, paragraph 2 allows the United States to tax only the lesser of two amounts of income: the amount determined by applying U.S. rules regarding the calculation of effectively connected income and the amount determined under Article 7 of the Convention. That is, a taxpayer may choose the set of rules that results in the lowest amount of taxable income, but may not combine both treaty and Code rules in a way that would be inconsistent with the intent of either set of rules.

Because the purpose of paragraph 2 is to determine the profits that are attributable to a permanent establishment, paragraph 2 applies in place only of Code section 864(c), which has an analogous function. The amount of income "attributable to" a permanent establishment under Article 7 may be greater or lesser than the amount of income that would be treated as "effectively connected" to a U.S. trade or business under section 864. Moreover, the profits attributable to a permanent establishment may be from sources within or without a Contracting State. However, as stated in paragraph 2, the business profits attributable to a permanent establishment include only those profits derived from the functions performed, assets used and risks assumed by the permanent establishment. For example, a foreign corporation that has a significant amount of third party foreign source royalty income attributable to a U.S. permanent establishment may find that it will pay less tax in the United States by applying section 864(c) of the Code, rather than Article 7, if the royalty income is not derived in the active conduct of a trade or business in the United States under Code section 864(c)(4)(B)(i). But, as described in the Technical Explanation to paragraph 2 of Article 1 (General Scope), if the foreign corporation chooses to apply Code Section 864(c) to determine its effectively connected income, it may not also use Article 7 principles to reduce its third party royalty income by interbranch royalty expense, since doing so would be inconsistent with either the principles of the Code or the Convention. (*See* Rev. Rul. 84-17, 1984-1 C.B. 308.). Conversely, if the taxpayer opts to use Article 7 to calculate the amount of business profits attributable to its U.S. permanent establishment, it must include all foreign-source income, from third parties and interbranch income in its business profits whether or not such income would be effectively connected income under the Code, if attributable to functions performed, assets used or risks assumed by the permanent establishment. Then, as stated above, the foreign corporation may elect to be taxed on the lower of the two amounts. Article 7 can only be used to reduce the amount of tax that would have otherwise been calculated using Code section 864(c) principles.

Paragraph 2 refers specifically to the dealings between the permanent establishment and other parts of the enterprise of which the permanent establishment is a part in order to emphasize that the separate and independent enterprise fiction of the paragraph requires that these dealings be treated the same way as similar transactions taking place between independent enterprises. That specific reference to dealings between the permanent establishment and other parts of the enterprise does not, however, restrict the scope of the paragraph. Where a transaction that takes place between the enterprise and an associated enterprise affects directly the determination of the profits attributable to the permanent establishment (*e.g.* the acquisition by the permanent establishment from an associated enterprise of goods that will be sold through the permanent establishment), paragraph 2 also requires that, for the purpose of computing the profits attributable to the permanent establishment, the conditions of the transaction be adjusted, if necessary, to reflect the conditions of a similar transaction between independent enterprises. Assume, for instance, that the permanent establishment situated in State S of an enterprise of State R acquires property from an associated enterprise of State T. If the price provided for in the contract between the two associated enterprises exceeds what would have been agreed to between independent enterprises, paragraph 2 of Article 7 of the treaty between State R and State S will authorize State S to adjust the profits attributable to the permanent establishment to reflect what a separate and independent enterprise would have paid for the property. In such case, Sate R will also be able to adjust the profits of the enterprise of State R under paragraph 1 of Article 9 of the treaty between State R and State T, which will trigger the application of the corresponding adjustment mechanism of paragraph 2 of Article 9 of that treaty.

Computation of the profits attributable to a permanent establishment under paragraph 2 takes into account the profits from all its activities, transactions with both associated and independent enterprises, and dealings with other parts of the enterprise. This analysis involves two steps. The first step requires a functional factual analysis to determine:

- the attribution to the permanent establishment of the rights and obligations arising out of transactions between the enterprise of which the permanent establishment is a part and separate enterprises;

- the identification of significant people functions relevant to the attribution of economic ownership of assets, and the attribution of economic ownership of assets to the permanent establishment;

- the identification of significant people functions relevant to the assumption of risks, and the attribution of risks to the permanent establishment;

- the identification of other functions of the permanent establishment;

- the recognition of dealings between the permanent establishment and other parts of the enterprise; and

- the attribution of capital based on the assets and risks attributed to the permanent establishment.

The second step is to price any such dealings that arc attributed to the permanent establishment in accordance with the 2010 Report. Thus, any of the methods permitted in the 2010 Report, including profits methods, may be used as appropriate and in accordance with the principles of the OECD's Transfer Pricing Guidelines. However, the attribution methods apply only for purposes of attributing profits within the legal entity. It does not create legal obligations or other tax consequences that would result from transactions having independent legal significance. In order to facilitate the administration of the two step process, taxpayers are encouraged to provide documentation supporting the conclusions reached in the first step, and demonstrating the appropriateness of the dealings and the associated prices.

An entity that operates through branches rather than separate subsidiaries will typically have lower capital requirements because the capital of the entity is available to support all of the entity's liabilities (with some exceptions attributable to local regulatory restrictions). This is the reason most commercial banks and some insurance companies operate through branches rather than through subsidiaries. The benefit that comes from such lower capital costs must be allocated among the branches in an appropriate manner. This issue does not arise in the case of an enterprise that operates through separate entities, since each entity will have to be separately capitalized or will have to compensate another entity for providing capital (usually through a guarantee).

Under U.S. domestic regulations, internal "transactions" generally are not recognized because they do not have legal significance. In contrast, paragraph 2 provides that such internal dealings may be used to allocate income in cases where the dealings accurately reflect the allocation of risk within the enterprise. One example is global trading in securities. In many cases, banks use internal swap transactions to transfer risk from one branch to a central location where traders have the expertise to manage that particular type of risk. Under the Convention, such a bank may also use such swap transactions as a means of allocating income between the branches, if use of that method is the "best method" within the meaning of regulation section 1.482-1(c). The books of a branch will not be respected, however, when the results are inconsistent with a functional analysis. So, for example, income from a transaction that is booked in a particular branch (or home office) will not be treated as attributable to that location if the sales and risk management functions that generate the income are performed in another location.

In the case of financial institutions, the use of internal dealings to allocate income within an enterprise may produce results under Article 7 that are significantly different than the results under the effectively connected income rules of Code section 864(c). For example, income from interbranch notional principal contracts may be taken into account under Article 7, notwithstanding that such transactions may be ignored for purposes of U.S. domestic law. Under the consistency rule described above, a financial institution that conducts different lines of business through its U.S. permanent establishment may not choose to apply the rules of the Code with respect to some lines of business and Article 7 of the Convention with respect to others. If it chooses to use the rules of Article 7 to allocate its income from its trading book, it may not then use U.S. domestic rules to allocate income from its loan portfolio.

Paragraph 2 provides that deductions shall be allowed for expenses incurred for purposes of a permanent establishment, ensuring that business profits will be taxed on a net basis. These deductions may include compensation to other parts of the enterprise for functions performed for the branch's benefit, if they are functions that would be compensated at arm's length. Thus, deductions against business profits may be allowed when an accounting unit of the enterprise books third-party expenses for purposes of the permanent establishment. However, the amount deducted to determine net business profits is not the actual amount of third-party expense booked, but rather the amount of compensation that would be paid at arm's length by the branch for the function performed.

For example, when the home office of an enterprise books interest expense that is used in part to fund the permanent establishment, the permanent establishment may deduct an arm's length amount of interest paid to the home office to compensate it for an appropriate amount of debt-funding. The permanent establishment may also take into account arm's length fees to an enterprise's treasury center for functions performed for its benefit. In each case, the amount of expense allowed as a deduction is determined by applying the arm's length principle. Similarly, where the branch and other parts of the enterprise share benefits of centralized functions, such as research and development or headquarters services, the deduction allowed to the permanent establishment would be its appropriate share of the arm's length compensation for such shared functions. The method to be used in calculating that compensation, and the permanent establishment's appropriate share thereof, will depend on the facts and circumstances, including the terms of the arrangements between the branches and head office. The amount of deduction could be computed as a share of either the total costs, or other value indicator, of the centralized function, depending on which provides the most reliable measure of the arm's length charge for sharing in the centralized functions in the facts and circumstances. The permanent establishment's appropriate share of such compensation for these functions will depend on the benefits it reasonably expects to receive from the arrangement as a proportion of the total reasonably expected benefits of all parts of the enterprise.

A permanent establishment cannot be funded entirely with debt, and must have sufficient capital to carry on its activities as if it were a distinct and separate enterprise. To the extent that the permanent establishment has not booked adequate capital, a Contracting State may attribute such capital to the permanent establishment and deny an interest deduction to the extent necessary to reflect that capital attribution. The method prescribed by U.S. domestic law for making this attribution is found in Treas. Reg. 1.882-5. Both Treas. Reg. 1.882-5 and the method prescribed in this paragraph start from the premise that all of the capital of the enterprise supports all of the assets and risks of the enterprise, and therefore the entire capital of the enterprise must be allocated to its various businesses and offices.

However, Treas. Reg. 1.882-5 does not take into account the fact that there is more risk associated with some assets than others. For instance, an independent enterprise would need less capital to support a floating rate U.S. Treasury security than it would need to support an equity security or other asset with significant market and/or credit risk. Accordingly, in some cases Treas. Reg. 1.882-5 would require a taxpayer to allocate more capital to the United States, and therefore would reduce the taxpayer's interest deduction more, than is appropriate. To address these cases, the Convention allows a taxpayer to apply a more flexible approach that takes into account the relative risk of its assets in the various jurisdictions in which it does business. In particular, in the case of financial institutions other than insurance companies, the amount of capital attributable to a permanent establishment is determined by allocating the institution's total capital between its offices on the basis of the proportion of the financial institution's risk-weighted assets attributable to each office. This recognizes the fact that financial institutions are in many cases required to risk-weight their assets for regulatory purposes and, in other cases, will do so for business reasons even if not required to do so by regulators. However, risk-weighting is more complicated than the method prescribed by Treas. Reg. 1.882-5. Accordingly, to ease this administrative burden, taxpayers may choose to apply the principles of Treas. Reg. 1.882-5(c) to determine the amount of capital allocable to its U.S. permanent establishment, in lieu of determining its allocable capital under the risk-weighted capital allocation method provided by the Convention, even if it has otherwise chosen to apply the principles of Article 7 rather than the effectively connected income rules of U.S. domestic law.

*Paragraph 3*

Paragraph 3 provides that where, in accordance with paragraph 2, a Contracting State adjusts the profits that are attributable to a permanent establishment of an enterprise of one of the Contracting States and taxes accordingly profits of the enterprise that have been charged to tax in the other State, the other Contracting State shall, to the extent necessary to eliminate double taxation, make an appropriate adjustment if it agrees with the adjustment made by the first-mentioned State. If the other Contracting state does not so agree, the Contracting States shall eliminate any double taxation resulting therefrom by mutual agreement.

*Paragraph 4*

Paragraph 4 coordinates the provisions of Article 7 and other provisions of the Convention. Under this paragraph, when business profits include items of income that are dealt with separately under other articles of the Convention, the provisions of those articles will, except when they specifically provide to the contrary, take precedence over the provisions of Article 7. For example, the taxation of dividends will be determined by the rules of Article 10 (Dividends), and not by Article 7, except where, as provided in paragraph 6 of Article 10, the dividend is attributable to a permanent establishment. In the latter case the provisions of Article 7 apply. Thus, an enterprise of one State deriving dividends from the other State may not rely on Article 7 to exempt those dividends from tax at source if they are not attributable to a permanent establishment of the enterprise in the other State. By the same token, if the dividends are attributable to a permanent establishment in the other State, the dividends may be taxed on a net income basis at the source State full corporate tax rate, rather than on a gross basis under Article 10.

As provided in Article 8 (Shipping and Air Transport), income derived from shipping and air transport activities in international traffic described in that Article is taxable only in the country of residence of the enterprise regardless of whether it is attributable to a permanent establishment situated in the source State.

*Paragraph 5*

Paragraph 5 incorporates into the Convention the principles of Code section 864(c)(6), but not section 864(c)(7). Like the Code section on which it is based, paragraph 5 provides that any income or gain attributable to a permanent establishment during its existence, following the rules of paragraph 2 and 3, is taxable in the Contracting State where the permanent establishment is situated, even if the payment of that income or gain is deferred until after the permanent establishment ceases to exist. This rule applies with respect to paragraphs 1 and 2 of Article 7 (Business Profits), paragraph 6 of Article 10 (Dividends), paragraph 6 of Article 11 (Interest), paragraph 4 of Articles 13 (Royalties) and 14 (Gains) and paragraph 2 of Article 21 (Other Income).

The effect of this rule can be illustrated by the following example. Assume a company that is a resident of the other Contracting State and that maintains a permanent establishment in the United States winds up the permanent establishment's business and sells the permanent establishment's inventory to a U.S. buyer prior to winding up in exchange for an interest-bearing installment obligation payable in full at the end of year 3.  Despite the fact that Article 14's threshold requirement for U.S. taxation is not met in year 3 because the company has no permanent establishment in the United States, the United States may tax the deferred income recognized by the company in year 3.

*Relationship to Other Articles*

This Article is subject to the saving clause of paragraph 4 of Article 1 (General Scope) of the Model.  Thus, if a citizen of the United States who is a resident of the other Contracting State under the treaty derives business profits from the United States that are not attributable to a permanent establishment in the United States, the United States may, subject to the special foreign tax credit rules of paragraph 4 of Article 23 (Relief from Double Taxation), tax those profits, notwithstanding the provision of paragraph 1 of this Article which would exempt the income from U.S. tax.

The benefits of this Article are also subject to Article 22 (Limitation on Benefits).  Thus, an enterprise of the other Contracting State and that derives income effectively connected with a U.S. trade or business may not claim the benefits of Article 7 unless the resident carrying on the enterprise qualifies for such benefits under Article 22.


## ARTICLE 8 (SHIPPING AND AIR TRANSPORT)

This Article governs the taxation of profits from the operation of ships and aircraft in international traffic.  The term "international traffic" is defined in subparagraph 1(f) of Article 3 (General Definitions).

*Paragraph 1*

Paragraph 1 provides that profits derived by an enterprise of a Contracting State from the operation in international traffic of ships or aircraft are taxable only in that Contracting State. Because paragraph 4 of Article 7 (Business Profits) defers to Article 8 with respect to taxation of shipping income, such income derived by a resident of one of the Contracting States may not be taxed in the other State even if the enterprise has a permanent establishment in that other State. Thus, if a U.S. airline has a ticket office in Poland, Poland may not tax the airline's profits attributable to that office under Article 7.  Since entities engaged in international transportation activities normally will have many permanent establishments in a number of countries, the rule avoids difficulties that would be encountered in attributing income to multiple permanent establishments if the income were covered by Article 7.

*Paragraph 2*

The income from the operation of ships or aircraft in international traffic that is exempt from tax under paragraph 1 is defined in paragraph 2.

In addition to income derived directly from the operation of ships and aircraft in international traffic, this definition also includes certain items of rental income. First, income of an enterprise of a Contracting State from the rental of ships or aircraft on a full basis (i.e., with crew) is income of the lessor from the operation of ships and aircraft in international traffic and, therefore, is exempt from tax in the other Contracting State under paragraph 1. Also, paragraph 2 encompasses income from the lease of ships or aircraft on a bareboat basis (i.e., without crew), either when the income is incidental to other income of the lessor from the operation of ships or aircraft in international traffic, or when the ships or aircraft are operated in international traffic by the lessee. If neither of those two conditions apply, income from the bareboat rentals would constitute business profits. The coverage of Article 8 is therefore broader than that of Article 8 of the OECD Model, which covers bareboat leasing only when it is incidental to other income of the lessor from the operation of ships of aircraft in international traffic.

Paragraph 2 also clarifies, consistent with the Commentary to Article 8 of the OECD Model, that income earned by an enterprise from the inland transport of property or passengers within either Contracting State falls within Article 8 if the transport is undertaken as part of the international transport of property or passengers by the enterprise. Thus, if a U.S. shipping company contracts to carry property from Poland to a U.S. city and, as part of that contract, it transports the property by truck from its point of origin to an airport in Poland (or it contracts with a trucking company to carry the property to the airport) the income earned by the U.S. shipping company from the overland leg of the journey would be taxable only in the United States. Similarly, Article 8 also would apply to all of the income derived from a contract for the international transport of goods, even if the goods were transported to the port by a lighter, not by the vessel that carried the goods in international waters.

Finally, certain non-transport activities that are an integral part of the services performed by a transport company, or are ancillary to the enterprise's operation of ships or aircraft in international traffic, are understood to be covered in paragraph 1, though they are not specified in paragraph 2. These include, for example, the provision of goods and services by engineers, ground and equipment maintenance and staff, cargo handlers, catering staff and customer services personnel. Where the enterprise provides such goods to, or performs services for, other enterprises and such activities are directly connected with or ancillary to the enterprise's operation of ships or aircraft in international traffic, the profits from the provision of such goods and services to other enterprises will fall under this paragraph.

For example, enterprises engaged in the operation of ships or aircraft in international traffic may enter into pooling arrangements for the purposes of reducing the costs of maintaining facilities needed for the operation of their ships or aircraft in other countries. For instance, where an airline enterprise agrees (for example, under an International Airlines Technical Pool agreement) to provide spare parts or maintenance services to other airlines landing at a particular location (which allows it to benefit from these services at other locations), activities carried on pursuant to that agreement will be ancillary to the operation of aircraft in international traffic by the enterprise.

Also, advertising that the enterprise may do for other enterprises in magazines offered aboard ships or aircraft that it operates in international traffic or at its business locations, such as ticket offices, is ancillary to its operation of these ships or aircraft. Profits generated by such

28

advertising fall within this paragraph. Income earned by concessionaires, however, is not covered by Article 8. These interpretations of paragraph 1 also are consistent with the Commentary to Article 8 of the OECD Model.

*Paragraph 3*

Under this paragraph, profits of an enterprise of a Contracting State from the use, maintenance or rental of containers (including equipment for their transport) are exempt from tax in the other Contracting State if such use, maintenance or rental, as the case may be, is incidental to the operation of ships or aircraft in international traffic. This treatment is consistent with the Commentary to Article 8 of the OECD Model, although it is narrower than the treatment under the U.S. Model, which provides for exclusive residence tax of such profits regardless of whether the recipient of the income is engaged in the operation of ships or aircraft in international traffic, and regardless of whether the enterprise has a permanent establishment in the other Contracting State.

*Paragraph 4*

This paragraph clarifies that the provisions of paragraphs 1 and 3 also apply to profits derived by an enterprise of a Contracting State from participation in a pool, joint business or international operating agency. This refers to various arrangements for international cooperation by carriers in shipping and air transport. For example, airlines from two countries may agree to share the transport of passengers between the two countries. They each will fly the same number of flights per week and share the revenues from that route equally, regardless of the number of passengers that each airline actually transports. Paragraph 4 makes clear that with respect to each carrier the income dealt with in the Article corresponds to that carrier's share of the total transport, not the income derived from the passengers actually carried by the airline. This paragraph corresponds to paragraph 4 of Article 8 of the OECD Model.

*Relationship to Other Articles*

The taxation of gains from the alienation of ships, aircraft or containers is not dealt with in this Article but in paragraph 5 of Article 14 (Capital Gains).

As with other benefits of the Convention, the benefit of exclusive residence country taxation under Article 8 is available to an enterprise only if it is entitled to benefits under Article 22 (Limitation on Benefits).

This Article also is subject to the saving clause of paragraph 4 of Article 1 (General Scope) of the Model. Thus, if a citizen of the United States who is a resident of Poland derives profits from the operation of ships or aircraft in international traffic, notwithstanding the exclusive residence country taxation in paragraph 1 of Article 8, the United States may, subject to the special foreign tax credit rules of paragraph 4 of Article 23 (Relief from Double Taxation), tax those profits as part of the worldwide income of the citizen. (This is an unlikely situation, however, because non-tax considerations (*e.g.*, insurance) generally result in shipping activities being carried on in corporate form.)

## ARTICLE 9 (ASSOCIATED ENTERPRISES)

This Article incorporates into the Convention the arm's-length principle reflected in the U.S. domestic transfer pricing provisions, particularly Code section 482. It provides that when related enterprises engage in a transaction on terms that are not arm's-length, the Contracting States may make appropriate adjustments to the taxable income and tax liability of such related enterprises to reflect what the income and tax of these enterprises with respect to the transaction would have been had there been an arm's-length relationship between them.

*Paragraph 1*

This paragraph is essentially the same as its counterpart in the OECD Model. It addresses the situation where an enterprise of a Contracting State is related to an enterprise of the other Contracting State, and there are arrangements or conditions imposed between the enterprises in their commercial or financial relations that are different from those that would have existed in the absence of the relationship. Under these circumstances, the Contracting States may adjust the income (or loss) of the enterprise to reflect what it would have been in the absence of such a relationship.

The paragraph identifies the relationships between enterprises that serve as a prerequisite to application of the Article. As the Commentary to the OECD Model makes clear, the necessary element in these relationships is effective control, which is also the standard for purposes of Code section 482. Thus, the Article applies if an enterprise of one State participates directly or indirectly in the management, control, or capital of the enterprise of the other State. Also, the Article applies if any third person or persons participate directly or indirectly in the management, control or capital of enterprises of different States. For this purpose, all types of control are included, *i.e.*, whether or not legally enforceable and however exercised or exercisable.

The fact that a transaction is entered into between such related enterprises does not, in and of itself, mean that a Contracting State may adjust the income (or loss) of one or both of the enterprises under the provisions of this Article. If the conditions of the transaction are consistent with those that would be made between independent persons, the income arising from that transaction should not be subject to adjustment under this Article.

Similarly, the fact that associated enterprises may have concluded arrangements, such as cost sharing arrangements or general services agreements, is not in itself an indication that the two enterprises have entered into a non-arm's-length transaction that should give rise to an adjustment under paragraph 1. Both related and unrelated parties enter into such arrangements (*e.g.*, joint venturers may share some development costs). As with any other kind of transaction, when related parties enter into an arrangement, the specific arrangement must be examined to see whether or not it meets the arm's-length standard. In the event that it does not, an appropriate adjustment may be made, which may include modifying the terms of the agreement or re-characterizing the transaction to reflect its substance.

It is understood that the Code section 482 "commensurate with income" standard for determining appropriate transfer prices for intangibles operates consistently with the arm's-length standard. The implementation of this standard in the regulations under Code section 482 is in accordance with the general principles of paragraph 1 of Article 9 of the Convention, as interpreted by the OECD Transfer Pricing Guidelines.

This Article also permits tax authorities to deal with thin capitalization issues. They may, in the context of Article 9, scrutinize more than the rate of interest charged on a loan between related persons. They also may examine the capital structure of an enterprise, whether a payment in respect of that loan should be treated as interest, and, if it is treated as interest, under what circumstances interest deductions should be allowed to the payor. Paragraph 2 of the Commentary to Article 9 of the OECD Model, together with the U.S. observation set forth in paragraph 15, sets forth a similar understanding of the scope of Article 9 in the context of thin capitalization.

*Paragraph 2*

When a Contracting State has made an adjustment that is consistent with the provisions of paragraph 1, and the other Contracting State agrees that the adjustment was appropriate to reflect arm's-length conditions, that other Contracting State is obligated to make a correlative adjustment (sometimes referred to as a "corresponding adjustment") to the tax liability of the related person in that other Contracting State. Although the OECD Model does not specify that the other Contracting State must agree with the initial adjustment before it is obligated to make the correlative adjustment, the Commentary makes clear that the paragraph is to be read as such.

As explained in the Commentary to Article 9 of the OECD Model, Article 9 leaves the treatment of "secondary adjustments" to the laws of the Contracting States. When an adjustment under Article 9 has been made, one of the parties will have in its possession funds that it would not have had at arm's length. The question arises as to how to treat these funds. In the United States the general practice is to treat such funds as a dividend or contribution to capital, depending on the relationship between the parties. Under certain circumstances, the parties may be permitted to restore the funds to the party that would have the funds had the transactions been entered into on arm's length terms, and to establish an account payable pending restoration of the funds. *See* Rev. Proc. 99-32, 1999-2 C.B. 296.

The Contracting State making a secondary adjustment will take the other provisions of the Convention, where relevant, into account. For example, if the effect of a secondary adjustment is to treat a U.S. corporation as having made a distribution of profits to its parent corporation in the other Contracting State, the provisions of Article 10 (Dividends) will apply, and the United States may impose a 5 percent withholding tax on the dividend. Also, if under Article 23 (Elimination of Double Taxation), Poland generally gives a credit for taxes paid with respect to such dividends, it would also be required to do so in this case.

The competent authorities are authorized by paragraph 3 of Article 25 (Mutual Agreement Procedure) to consult, if necessary, to resolve any differences in the application of these provisions. For example, there may be a disagreement over whether an adjustment made by

31

a Contracting State under paragraph 1 was appropriate.

If a correlative adjustment is made under paragraph 2, it is to be implemented, pursuant to paragraph 2 of Article 25 (Mutual Agreement Procedure), notwithstanding any time limits or other procedural limitations in the law of the Contracting State making the adjustment. Thus, even if a statute of limitations has expired, a refund of tax can be made in order to implement a correlative adjustment (statutory or procedural limitations, however, cannot be overridden to impose additional tax, pursuant to paragraph 2 of Article 1 (General Scope)). If a taxpayer has entered a closing agreement (or other written settlement) with the United States prior to bringing a case to the competent authorities, the U.S. competent authority will endeavor only to obtain a correlative adjustment from the other Contracting State. *See* Rev Proc. 2006-54, 2006-2 C.B. 1035, § 7.05 (or any applicable successor procedures).

*Relationship to Other Articles*

The saving clause of paragraph 4 of Article 1 does not apply to paragraph 2 of Article 9 by virtue of an exception to the saving clause in subparagraph 5(a) of Article 1. This permits the competent authorities of the Contracting States to make any adjustments necessary to relieve double taxation pursuant to the mutual agreement procedure.

## ARTICLE 10 (DIVIDENDS)

Article 10 provides rules for the taxation of dividends paid by a company that is a resident of one Contracting State to a beneficial owner that is a resident of the other Contracting State. The Article provides for full residence-State taxation of such dividends and a limited source-State right to tax. Article 10 also provides rules for the imposition of a tax on branch profits by the State of source. Finally, the Article prohibits a State from imposing taxes on a company resident in the other Contracting State, other than a branch profits tax as provided in Article 12 (Branch Profits), on undistributed earnings.

*Paragraph 1*

Paragraph 1 permits a Contracting State to tax its residents on dividends paid to them by a company that is a resident of the other Contracting State. For dividends from any other source paid to a resident, Article 21 (Other Income) grants the residence country exclusive taxing jurisdiction (other than for dividends attributable to a permanent establishment in the other State).

*Paragraph 2*

The State of source also may tax dividends beneficially owned by a resident of the other State, subject to the limitations of paragraphs 2 and 3. Paragraph 2 generally limits the rate of withholding tax in the State of source on dividends paid by a company resident in that State to 15 percent of the gross amount of the dividend. If, however, the beneficial owner of the dividend is a company resident in the other State and owns directly shares representing at least 10 percent of the voting power of the company paying the dividend, then the rate of withholding tax in the

State of source is limited to 5 percent of the gross amount of the dividend. For application of this paragraph by the United States, shares are considered voting stock if they provide the power to elect, appoint or replace any person vested with the powers ordinarily exercised by the board of directors of a U.S. corporation.

The determination of whether the ownership threshold for subparagraph 2(a) is met for purposes of the 5 percent maximum rate of withholding tax is made on the date on which entitlement to the dividend is determined. Thus, in the case of a dividend from a U.S. company, the determination of whether the ownership threshold is met generally would be made on the dividend record date.

Paragraph 2 does not affect the taxation of the profits out of which the dividends are paid. The taxation by a Contracting State of the income of its resident companies is governed by the domestic law of the Contracting State, subject to the provisions of paragraph 4 of Article 24 (Non-Discrimination).

The term "beneficial owner" is not defined in the Convention, and is, therefore, generally defined under the domestic law of the country imposing tax (*i.e.*, the source country). The beneficial owner of the dividend for purposes of Article 10 is the person to which the income is attributable under the laws of the source State. Thus, if a dividend paid by a corporation that is a resident of one of the States (as determined under Article 4 (Residence)) is received by a nominee or agent that is a resident of the other State on behalf of a person that is not a resident of that other State, the dividend is not entitled to the benefits of this Article. However, a dividend received by a nominee on behalf of a resident of that other State would be entitled to benefits. These limitations are confirmed by paragraphs 12-12.2 of the Commentary to Article 10 of the OECD Model.

Special rules apply to shares held through fiscally transparent entities both for purposes of determining whether the ownership threshold has been met and for purposes of determining the beneficial owner of the dividend.

A company that is a resident of a Contracting State shall be considered to own directly the voting stock owned by an entity that is considered fiscally transparent under the laws of that State and that is not a resident of the other Contracting State of which the company paying the dividends is a resident, in proportion to the company's ownership interest in that entity. This is consistent with the rules of paragraph 6 of Article 1 (General Scope), which provides that residence State principles shall be used to determine who derives the dividends, to assure that the dividends for which the source State grants benefits of the Convention will be taken into account for tax purposes by a resident of the residence State.

For example, assume that FCo, a company that is a resident of Poland, owns a 50 percent interest in FP, a partnership that is organized in Poland. FP owns 100 percent of the sole class of stock of USCo, a company resident in the United States. Poland views FP as fiscally transparent under its domestic law, and taxes FCo currently on its distributive share of the income of FP and determines the character and source of the income received through FP in the hands of FCo as if such income were realized directly by FCo. In this case, FCo is treated as deriving 50 percent of the dividends paid by USCo under paragraph 6 of Article 1. Moreover, FCo is treated as owning 50 percent of the stock of USCo directly. The same result would be reached even if the tax laws of the United States would treat FP differently (*e.g.*, if FP were not treated as fiscally transparent in the United States). If FP were organized in a third state, is not viewed as fiscally transparent under U.S. law, and would be eligible for benefits with respect to the dividend under a tax treaty between the United States and the third state, paragraph 6 of Article 1 provides that FCo is treated as deriving 50 percent of the dividends paid by USCo only if the applicable dividend withholding rate provided under the Convention (5 percent) is more favorable than the applicable dividend withholding rate that FP could claim with respect to the dividend in its own right under the tax treaty between the United States and the third country.

While residence State principles control who is treated as owning voting stock of the company paying dividends through a fiscally transparent entity and, consequently, who derives the dividends, source State principles of beneficial ownership apply to determine whether the person who derives the dividends, or another resident of the other Contracting State, is the beneficial owner of the dividends. If the person who derives the dividends under paragraph 6 of Article 1 would not be treated as a nominee, agent, custodian, conduit, etc. under the source State's principles for determining beneficial ownership, that person will be treated as the beneficial owner of the dividends for purposes of the Convention. In the example above, FCo is required to satisfy the beneficial ownership principles of the United States with respect to the dividends it derives. If under the beneficial ownership principles of the United States, FCo is found not to be the beneficial owner of the dividends, FCo will not be entitled to the benefits of Article 10 with respect to such dividends. If FCo is found to be a nominee, agent, custodian, or conduit for a person who is a resident of Poland, that person may be entitled to benefits with respect to the dividends.

*Paragraph 3*

Paragraph 3 provides that dividends beneficially owned by a pension fund may not be taxed in the Contracting State of which the company paying the tax is a resident, unless such dividends are derived from the carrying on of a business, directly or indirectly, by the pension fund or through an associated enterprise. For purposes of application of this paragraph by the United States, the term "trade or business" shall be defined in accordance with Code section 513(c). The term "pension fund" is defined in subparagraph 1(k) of Article 3 (General Definitions).

*Paragraph 4*

Paragraph 4 imposes limitations on the rate reductions provided by paragraphs 2 and 3 in the case of dividends paid by a RIC or a REIT.

The first sentence of subparagraph 4(a) provides that dividends paid by a RIC or REIT are not eligible for the 5 percent rate of withholding tax of subparagraph 2(a).

The second sentence of subparagraph 4(a) provides that the 15 percent maximum rate of withholding tax of subparagraph 2(b) applies to dividends paid by RICs and that the elimination of source-country withholding tax of paragraph 3 applies to dividends paid by RICs and beneficially owned by a pension fund.

The third sentence of subparagraph 4(a) provides that the 15 percent rate of withholding tax also applies to dividends paid by a REIT and that the elimination of source-country withholding tax of paragraph 3 applies to dividends paid by REITs and beneficially owned by a pension fund, provided that one of the three following conditions is met. First, the beneficial owner of the dividend is an individual or a pension fund, in either case holding an interest of not more than 10 percent in the REIT. Second, the dividend is paid with respect to a class of stock that is publicly traded and the beneficial owner of the dividend is a person holding an interest of not more than 5 percent of any class of the REIT's shares. Third, the beneficial owner of the dividend holds an interest in the REIT of not more than 10 percent and the REIT is "diversified."

Subparagraph 4(b) provides a definition of the term "diversified." A REIT is diversified if the gross value of no single interest in real property held by the REIT exceeds 10 percent of the gross value of the REIT's total interest in real property. Section 856(e) foreclosure property is not considered an interest in real property, and a REIT holding a partnership interest is treated as owning its proportionate share of any interest in real property held by the partnership.

Subparagraph 4(c) provides that the rules of paragraph 4 shall apply to dividends paid by companies resident in Poland that the competent authorities have determined by mutual agreement are similar to a RIC or a REIT.

*Paragraph 5*

Paragraph 5 defines the term dividends broadly and flexibly. The definition is intended to cover all arrangements that yield a return on an equity investment in a corporation as determined under the tax law of the state of source, as well as arrangements that might be developed in the future.

The term includes income from shares, or other corporate rights that are not treated as debt under the law of the source State, that participate in the profits of the company. The term also includes income that is subjected to the same tax treatment as income from shares by the law of the State of source. Thus, a constructive dividend that results from a non-arm's length transaction between a corporation and a related party is a dividend. In the case of the United States the term dividend includes amounts treated as a dividend under U.S. law upon the sale or redemption of shares or upon a transfer of shares in a reorganization. *See* Rev. Rul. 92-85, 1992-2 C.B. 69 (sale of foreign subsidiary's stock to U.S. sister company is a deemed dividend to extent of the subsidiary's and sister company's earnings and profits). Further, a distribution from a U.S. publicly traded limited partnership, which is taxed as a corporation under U.S. law, is a dividend for purposes of Article 10. However, a distribution by a limited liability company is not taxable by the United States under Article 10, provided the limited liability company is not characterized as an association taxable as a corporation under U.S. law.

Finally, a payment denominated as interest that is made by a thinly capitalized corporation may be treated as a dividend to the extent that the debt is recharacterized as equity under the laws of the source State.

*Paragraph 6*

Paragraph 6 provides a rule for taxing dividends paid with respect to holdings that form part of the business property of a permanent establishment. In such case, the rules of Article 7 (Business Profits) shall apply. Accordingly, the dividends will be taxed on a net basis using the rates and rules of taxation generally applicable to residents of the State in which the permanent establishment is located, as such rules may be modified by the Convention. An example of dividends paid with respect to the business property of a permanent establishment would be dividends derived by a dealer in stock or securities from stock or securities that the dealer held for sale to customers.

*Paragraph 7*

The right of a Contracting State to tax dividends paid by a company that is a resident of the other Contracting State is restricted by paragraph 7 to cases in which the dividends are paid to a resident of that Contracting State or are attributable to a permanent establishment in that Contracting State. Thus, a Contracting State may not impose a "secondary" withholding tax on dividends paid by a nonresident company out of earnings and profits from that Contracting State.

The paragraph also restricts the right of a Contracting State to impose corporate level taxes on undistributed profits, other than a branch profits tax. The paragraph does not restrict a State's right to tax its resident shareholders on undistributed earnings of a corporation resident in the other State. Thus, the authority of the United States to impose taxes on subpart F income and on earnings deemed invested in U.S. property, and its tax on income of a passive foreign investment company that is a qualified electing fund is in no way restricted by this provision.

*Relationship to Other Articles*

Notwithstanding the foregoing limitations on source country taxation of dividends, the saving clause of paragraph 4 of Article 1 permits the United States to tax its residents and citizens, subject to the special foreign tax credit rules of paragraph 4 of Article 23 (Elimination of Double Taxation), as if the Convention had not come into effect.

Rules regarding the application of branch profits taxes are found in Article 12 (Branch Profits).

The benefits of this Article are also subject to the provisions of Article 22 (Limitation on Benefits). Thus, if a resident of Poland is the beneficial owner of dividends paid by a U.S. corporation, that shareholder must qualify for treaty benefits under at least one of the tests of Article 22 in order to receive the benefits of this Article.

## ARTICLE 11 (INTEREST)

Article 11 specifies the taxing jurisdictions over interest income of the States of source and residence and defines the terms necessary to apply the Article.

*Paragraph 1*

Paragraph 1 grants the Contracting State of residence the non-exclusive right to tax interest beneficially owned by its residence and arising in the other Contracting State.

*Paragraph 2*

Paragraph 2 provides that the State of source may also tax interest beneficially owned by a resident of the other Contracting State, but limits the rate of tax to 5 percent of the gross amount of the interest.

The term "beneficial owner" is not defined in the Convention, and is, therefore, defined under the domestic law of the State of source. The beneficial owner of the interest for purposes of Article 11 is the person to which the income is attributable under the laws of the source State. Thus, if interest arising in a Contracting State is received by a nominee or agent that is a resident of the other State on behalf of a person that is not a resident of that other State, the interest is not entitled to the benefits of Article 11. However, interest received by a nominee on behalf of a resident of that other State would be entitled to benefits. These limitations are confirmed by paragraph 9 of the OECD Commentary to Article 11.

Special rules apply to interest derived through fiscally transparent entities for purposes of determining the beneficial owner of the interest. In such cases, residence State principles shall be used to determine who derives the interest, to assure that the interest for which the source State grants benefits of the Convention will be taken into account for tax purposes by a resident of the residence State.

For example, assume that FCo, a company that is a resident of Poland, owns a 50 percent interest in FP, a partnership that is organized in Poland. FP receives interest arising in the United States. Poland views FP as fiscally transparent under its domestic law, and taxes FCo currently on its distributive share of the income of FP and determines the character and source of the income received through FP in the hands of FCo as if such income were realized directly by FCo. In this case, FCo is treated as deriving 50 percent of the interest received by FP that arises in the United States under paragraph 6 of Article 1. The same result would be reached even if the tax laws of the United States would treat FP differently (*e.g.*, if FP were not treated as fiscally transparent in the United States). If FP were organized in a third state, were not viewed as fiscally transparent under U.S. law, and would be eligible for benefits with respect to the interest under a tax treaty between the United States and the third state, paragraph 6 of Article 1 provides that FCo is treated as deriving 50 percent of the interest paid by USCo only if the applicable interest withholding rate provided under the Convention is more favorable than the applicable interest withholding rate that FP could claim with respect to the interest in its own right under the tax treaty between the United States and the third country.

While residence State principles control who is treated as deriving the interest, source State principles of beneficial ownership apply to determine whether the person who derives the interest, or another resident of the other Contracting State, is the beneficial owner of the interest. If the person who derives the interest under paragraph 6 of Article 1 would not be treated as a nominee, agent, custodian, conduit, etc. under the source State's principles for determining beneficial ownership, that person will be treated as the beneficial owner of the interest for purposes of the Convention. In the example above, FCo is required to satisfy the beneficial ownership principles of the United States with respect to the interest it derives. If under the beneficial ownership principles of the United States, FCo is found not to be the beneficial owner of the interest, FCo will not be entitled to the benefits of Article 11 with respect to such interest. If FCo is found to be a nominee, agent, custodian, or conduit for a person who is a resident of Poland, that person may be entitled to benefits with respect to the interest.

*Paragraph 3*

Paragraph 3 provides that notwithstanding the provisions of paragraph 2, interest described in paragraph 1 shall be taxable only in the Contracting State in which the recipient is a resident if the beneficial owner of the interest is a resident of that State and either: (1) is that Contracting State or the central bank, a political subdivision, local authority or statutory body thereof; (2) the interest is paid by the Contracting State in which the interest arises or by the central bank, a political subdivision, local authority or statutory body thereof; (3) the interest is paid in respect of a loan, debt-claim or credit that is owed to, or made, provided, guaranteed or insured by that Contracting State or a political subdivision, local authority, statutory body or export financing agency thereof; (4) is a pension fund, but only if the pension fund does not derive the interest from the carrying on of a business, directly or indirectly, or is (5) either: (a) a bank; (b) an insurance company; (c) an enterprise (other than a bank) that is unrelated to the payer of the interest and that substantially derives its gross income from the active and regular conduct of a lending or finance business. Clause (iii) of subparagraph 3(e) provides the following non-exhaustive list of activities that for purposes of subparagraph 3(e) are considered a lending or finance business: (1) making loans; (2) purchasing or discounting accounts receivable, notes or installment obligations; (3) engaging in finance leasing (including purchasing, servicing, and disposing of finance leases and related leased assets); (4) issuing letters of credit or providing guarantees; or (5) providing charge and credit card services.

*Paragraph 4*

Paragraph 4 provides anti-abuse exceptions to paragraphs 2 and 3 for two classes of interest payments.

The first class of interest, dealt with in subparagraph 4(a), is so-called contingent interest. Under this provision, interest arising in one of the Contracting States that is determined with reference to receipts, sales, income, profits or other cash flows of the debtor or a related person, to any change in the value of any property of the debtor or a related person or to any dividend, partnership distribution or similar payment made by the debtor or a related person also may be taxed in the State in which it arises, and according to the laws of that State. If the beneficial owner is a resident of the other Contracting State, however, the gross amount of the interest may be taxed at a rate not exceeding 15 percent of the gross amount of the payment. With respect to such interest arising in the United States, subparagraph 4(a) refers to contingent interest of a type described in Code section 871(h)(4)(C), including the exceptions of that section where applicable.

The second class of interest that is dealt with in subparagraph 4(b), in the case of the United States, is excess inclusions from U.S. real estate mortgage investment conduits ("REMICs"). Subparagraph 4(b) serves as a backstop to Code section 860G(b). That section generally requires that a foreign person holding a residual interest in a REMIC take into account for U.S. tax purposes "any excess inclusion" and "amounts includible ... [under the REMIC provisions] when paid or distributed (or when the interest is disposed of)...."

Without a full tax at source, non-U.S. transferees of residual interests would have a competitive advantage over U.S. transferees at the time these interests are initially offered. Absent this rule, the United States would suffer a revenue loss with respect to mortgages held in a REMIC because of opportunities for tax avoidance created by differences in the timing of taxable and economic income produced by such interests. In many cases, the transfer to the foreign person is simply disregarded under Treas. Reg. 1.860G-3. Subparagraph 4(b) also provides that excess inclusions from REMICs are not considered "other income" subject to Article 21 (Other Income) of the Convention.

*Paragraph 5*

The term "interest" as used in Article 11 is defined in paragraph 5 to include, *inter alia*, income from debt claims of every kind, whether or not secured by a mortgage. Penalty charges for late payment are excluded from the definition of interest. Interest that is paid or accrued subject to a contingency is within the ambit of Article 11. This definition includes income from a debt obligation carrying the right to participate in profits. The term does not, however, include amounts treated as dividends under Article 10 (Dividends).

The term interest also includes amounts which under the taxation law of the Contracting State in which the income arises are assimilated to income from money lent. This wording is to be interpreted consistently with the U.S. Model reference to "amounts subject to the same tax treatment as income from money lent under the law of the State in which the income arises." Thus, for purposes of the Convention, amounts that the United States will treat as interest include (i) the difference between the issue price and the stated redemption price at maturity of a debt instrument (*i.e.*, original issue discount ("OID")), which may be wholly or partially realized on the disposition of a debt instrument (section 1273), (ii) amounts that are imputed interest on a deferred sales contract (section 483), (iii) amounts treated as interest or OID under the stripped bond rules (section 1286), (iv) amounts treated as original issue discount under the below-market interest rate rules (section 7872), (v) a partner's distributive share of a partnership's interest income (section 702), (vi) the interest portion of periodic payments made under a "finance lease" or similar contractual arrangement that in substance is a borrowing by the nominal lessee to finance the acquisition of property, (vii) amounts included in the income of a holder of a residual interest in a REMIC (section 860E), because these amounts generally are subject to the same taxation treatment as interest under U.S. tax law, and (viii) interest with respect to notional principal contracts that are recharacterized as loans because of a "substantial non-periodic payment."

*Paragraph 6*

Paragraph 6 provides an exception to paragraphs 1, 2 and 3 in cases where the beneficial owner of the interest carries on business through a permanent establishment situated in that State and the debt-claim in respect of which the interest is paid is effectively connected with such permanent establishment. In such cases the provisions of Article 7 (Business Profits) will apply and the State of source will retain the right to impose tax on such interest income.

In the case of a permanent establishment that once existed in a Contracting State but no longer exists, the provisions of this paragraph apply, by virtue of paragraph 5 of Article 7 (Business Profits), to interest paid with respect to a debt-claim that would be effectively connected to such a permanent establishment if it did exist in the year of payment or accrual. See the Technical Explanation of paragraph 5 of Article 7. Accordingly, such interest would remain taxable under the provisions of Article 7, and not under this Article.

*Paragraph 7*

Paragraph 7 provides a general source rule for interest. Interest is considered to arise in a Contracting State if paid by a resident of that State (including that State itself or one of its political subdivisions or local authorities). Interest that is borne by a permanent establishment in one of the Contracting States is considered to arise in that State. For this purpose, interest is considered to be borne by a permanent establishment if it is allocable to taxable income of that permanent establishment or fixed base. If the actual amount of interest on the books of a U.S. branch of a resident of Poland exceeds the amount of interest allocated to the branch under Treas. Reg. 1.882-5, the amount of such excess will not be considered U.S. source interest for purposes of this Article.

*Paragraph 8*

Paragraph 8 provides that in cases involving special relationships between the payer and the beneficial owner of interest income, Article 11 applies only to that portion of the total interest payments that would have been made absent such special relationships (*i.e.*, an arm's-length interest payment). Any excess amount of interest paid remains taxable according to the laws of the United States and the other Contracting State, respectively, with due regard to the other provisions of the Convention. Thus, if the excess amount would be treated under the source country's law as a distribution of profits by a corporation, such amount could be taxed as a dividend rather than as interest, but the tax would be subject, if appropriate, to the rate limitations of paragraph 2 of Article 10 (Dividends).

The term "special relationship" is not defined in the Convention. In applying this paragraph the United States considers the term to include the relationships described in Article 9, which in turn corresponds to the definition of "control" for purposes of Code section 482.

This paragraph does not address cases where, owing to a special relationship between the payer and the beneficial owner or between both of them and some other person, the amount of the interest is less than an arm's-length amount. In those cases a transaction may be characterized to reflect its substance and interest may be imputed consistent with the definition of "interest" in paragraph 3. The United States would apply Code section 482 or 7872 to determine the amount of imputed interest in those cases.

*Relationship to Other Articles*

Notwithstanding the foregoing limitations on source country taxation of interest, the saving clause of paragraph 4 of Article 1 permits the United States to tax its residents and citizens, subject to the special foreign tax credit rules of paragraph 4 of Article 23 (Relief from Double Taxation), as if the Convention had not come into force.

Rules regarding the application of branch-level interest taxes are found in Article 12 (Branch Profits).

As with other benefits of the Convention, the benefits of Article 11 are available to a resident of the other State only if that resident is entitled to those benefits under the provisions of Article 22 (Limitation on Benefits).

## ARTICLE 12 (BRANCH PROFITS)

*Paragraph 1*

Paragraph 1 permits a Contracting State to impose a branch profits tax on a company resident in the other Contracting State. The tax is in addition to other taxes permitted by the Convention. The term "company" is defined in subparagraph 1(b) of Article 3 (General Definitions).

A Contracting State may impose a branch profits tax on a company if the company has income attributable to a permanent establishment in that Contracting State, derives income from real property in that Contracting State that is taxed on a net basis under Article 6 (Income from Real Property), or realizes gains taxable in that State under paragraph 1 of Article 14 (Capital Gains). In the case of the United States, the imposition of such tax is limited, however, to the portion of the aforementioned items of income that represents the amount of such income that is the "dividend equivalent amount." This is consistent with the relevant rules under the U.S. branch profits tax, and the term dividend equivalent amount is defined under U.S. law. Section 884 defines the dividend equivalent amount as an amount for a particular year that is equivalent to the income described above that is included in the corporation's effectively connected earnings and profits for that year, after payment of the corporate tax under Articles 6, 7 (Business Profits) or 14, reduced for any increase in the branch's U.S. net equity during the year or increased for any reduction in its U.S. net equity during the year. U.S. net equity is U.S. assets less U.S. liabilities. *See* Treas. Reg. 1.884-1.

The dividend equivalent amount for any year approximates the dividend that a U.S. branch office would have paid during the year if the branch had been operated as a separate U.S. subsidiary company. In the case that Poland also imposes a branch profits tax, the base of its tax must be limited to an amount that is analogous to the dividend equivalent amount, and the applicable rate would be subject to the limitations of clause (ii) of subparagraph 1(b).

As discussed in the Technical Explanations to Articles 1(2) and 7(2), consistency principles prohibit a taxpayer from applying provisions of the Code and this Convention in an inconsistent manner in order to minimize tax. In the context of the branch profits tax, this consistency requirement means that if a company resident in Poland uses the principles of Article 7 to determine its U.S. taxable income, it must then also use those principles to determine its dividend equivalent amount. Similarly, if the company instead uses the Code to determine its U.S. taxable income it must also use the Code to determine its dividend equivalent amount. As in the case of Article 7, if a company of Poland, for example, does not from year to year consistently apply the Code or the Convention to determine its dividend equivalent amount, then the company must make appropriate adjustments or recapture amounts that would otherwise be subject to U.S. branch profits tax if it had consistently applied the Code or the Convention to determine its dividend equivalent amount from year to year.

Clause (ii) of subparagraph 1(b) provides that the branch profits tax shall not be imposed at a rate exceeding five percent, as provided in subparagraph 2(a) of Article 10 (Dividends). Subparagraph 1(b) applies equally if a taxpayer determines its taxable income under the laws of a Contracting State or under the provisions of Article 7. For example, as discussed above, consistency principles require a company resident in Poland that determines its U.S. taxable income under the Code to also determine its dividend equivalent amount under the Code. In that case, the withholding rate reduction provided in subparagraph 2(a) of Article 10 would apply even though the company did not determine its dividend equivalent amount using the principles of Article 7.

*Paragraph 2*

Paragraph 2 permits a Contracting State to impose its branch level interest tax on a company resident in the other Contracting State. The base of this tax is the excess, if any, of the interest allocable to the profits of the company that are either attributable to a permanent establishment in the first-mentioned State (including gains under paragraph 4 of Article 14 (Capital Gains)) or subject to tax in the first-mentioned State under Article 6 (Income from Real Property) or paragraph 1 of Article 14, over the interest paid on indebtedness related to that permanent establishment, or in the case of profits subject to tax under Article 6 or paragraph 1 of Article 14, over the interest paid by that trade or business in the first-mentioned State. Such excess interest may be taxed as if it were interest arising in the first-mentioned State and beneficially owned by the resident of the other State. Thus, such excess interest may be taxed by the first-mentioned State at a rate not to exceed the applicable rates provided in paragraph 2 of Article 11 (Interest).

*Relationship to Other Articles*

Notwithstanding the foregoing limitations on source country taxation, the saving clause of paragraph 4 of Article 1 permits the United States to tax its residents and citizens, subject to the special foreign tax credit rules of paragraph 4 of Article 23 (Relief from Double Taxation), as if the Convention had not come into effect.

The benefits of this Article are also subject to the provisions of Article 22 (Limitation on Benefits).

## ARTICLE 13 (ROYALTIES)

Article 13 provides rules for the taxation of royalties arising in one Contracting State and paid to a beneficial owner that is a resident of the other Contracting State.

*Paragraph 1*

Paragraph 1 grants to the State of residence the non-exclusive right to tax royalties beneficially owned by its residents and arising in the other Contracting State.

*Paragraph 2*

Paragraph 2 provides that the State of source may also tax royalties, but if the beneficial owner of the royalties is a resident of the other Contracting State, the rate of tax shall be limited to 5 percent of the gross amount of the royalties.

The term "beneficial owner" is not defined in the Convention, and is, therefore, defined under the domestic law of the State of source. The beneficial owner of the royalties for purposes of Article 13 is the person to which the income is attributable under the laws of the source State. Thus, if royalties arising in a Contracting State are received by a nominee or agent that is a resident of the other State on behalf of a person that is not a resident of that other State, the royalties are not entitled to the benefits of Article 13. However, the royalties received by a nominee on behalf of a resident of that other State would be entitled to benefits. These limitations are confirmed by paragraph 4 of the OECD Commentary to Article 12 of the OECD Model.

Special rules apply to royalties derived through fiscally transparent entities for purposes of determining the beneficial owner of the royalties. In such cases, residence State principles shall be used to determine who derives the royalties, to assure that the royalties for which the source State grants benefits of the Convention will be taken into account for tax purposes by a resident of the residence State.

For example, assume that FCo, a company that is a resident of Poland, owns a 50 percent interest in FP, a partnership that is organized in Poland. FP receives royalties arising in the United States. Poland views FP as fiscally transparent under its domestic law, and taxes FCo currently on its distributive share of the income of FP and determines the character and source of the income received through FP in the hands of FCo as if such income were realized directly by FCo. In this case, FCo is treated as deriving 50 percent of the royalties received by FP that arise in the United States under paragraph 6 of Article 1. The same result would be reached even if the tax laws of the United States would treat FP differently (*e.g.*, if FP were not treated as fiscally transparent in the United States). If FP were organized in a third state, were not viewed as fiscally transparent under U.S. law, and would be eligible for benefits with respect to the royalty under a tax treaty between the United States and the third state, paragraph 6 of Article 1 provides that FCo is treated as deriving 50 percent of the U.S.-source royalty only if the applicable royalty withholding rate provided under the Convention is more favorable than the applicable royalty withholding rate that FP could claim with respect to the royalty in its own right under the tax treaty between the United States and the third country.

While residence State principles control who is treated as deriving the royalties, source State principles of beneficial ownership apply to determine whether the person who derives the royalties, or another resident of the other Contracting State, is the beneficial owner of the royalties. If the person who derives the royalties under paragraph 6 of Article 1 would not be treated as a nominee, agent, custodian, conduit, etc. under the source State's principles for determining beneficial ownership, that person will be treated as the beneficial owner of the royalties for purposes of the Convention. In the example above, FCo is required to satisfy the beneficial ownership principles of the United States with respect to the royalties it derives. If under the beneficial ownership principles of the United States, FCo is found not to be the beneficial owner of the royalties, FCo will not be entitled to the benefits of Article 13 with respect to such royalties. If FCo is found to be a nominee, agent, custodian, or conduit for a person who is a resident of Poland, that person may be entitled to benefits with respect to the royalties.

*Paragraph 3*

Paragraph 3 defines the term "royalties," as used in Article 13 with an exhaustive list of examples. Subparagraph 3(a) first defines royalties to mean payments of any kind received as a consideration for the use of, or the right to use, any copyright of literary, artistic scientific or other work (including cinematographic films or radio or television broadcasting tapes), any patent, trademark, design or model, plan, secret formula or process, or for information concerning industrial, commercial, or scientific experience. Subparagraph 3(b) also provides that "royalties" also include gain derived from the alienation of any right or property that would give rise to royalties, to the extent the gain is contingent on the productivity, use, or further alienation thereof. Gains that are not so contingent are dealt with under Article 14 (Capital Gains). Lastly, subparagraph 3(c) provides that "royalties" also include payments of any kind received as a consideration for the use of, or the right to use any industrial, commercial, or scientific equipment.

The term royalties is defined in the Convention and therefore is generally independent of domestic law. Certain terms used in the definition are not defined in the Convention, but these may be defined under domestic tax law. For example, the term "secret process or formula" is found in the Code, and its meaning has been elaborated in the context of sections 351 and 367. *See* Rev. Rul. 55-17, 1955-1 C.B. 388; Rev. Rul. 64-56, 1964-1 C.B. 133; Rev. Proc. 69-19, 1969-2 C.B. 301.

Consideration for the use or right to use cinematographic films, or works on film, tape, or other means of reproduction in radio or television broadcasting is specifically included in the definition of royalties. It is intended that, with respect to any subsequent technological advances in the field of radio or television broadcasting, consideration received for the use of such technology will also be included in the definition of royalties.

If an artist who is resident in one Contracting State records a performance in the other Contracting State, retains a copyrighted interest in a recording, and receives payments for the right to use the recording based on the sale or public playing of the recording, then the right of such other Contracting State to tax those payments is governed by Article 13. *See* Boulez v. Commissioner, 83 T.C. 584 (1984), aff'd, 810 F.2d 209 (D.C. Cir. 1986). By contrast, if the artist earns in the other Contracting State income covered by Article 17 (Entertainers and Sportsmen), for example, endorsement income from the artist's attendance at a film screening, and if such income also is attributable to one of the rights described in Article 13 (*e.g.*, the use of the artist's photograph in promoting the screening), Article 17 and not Article 13 is applicable to such income.

Computer software generally is protected by copyright laws around the world. Under the Convention, consideration received for the use, or the right to use, computer software is treated either as royalties or as business profits, depending on the facts and circumstances of the transaction giving rise to the payment.

The primary factor in determining whether consideration received for the use, or the right to use, computer software is treated as royalties or as business profits is the nature of the rights transferred. *See* Treas. Reg. 1.861-18. The fact that the transaction is characterized as a license for copyright law purposes is not dispositive. For example, a typical retail sale of "shrink wrap" software generally will not be considered to give rise to royalty income, even though for copyright law purposes it may be characterized as a license.

The means by which the computer software is transferred are not relevant for purposes of the analysis. Consequently, if software is electronically transferred but the rights obtained by the transferee are substantially equivalent to rights in a program copy, the payment will be considered business profits.

The term "industrial, commercial, or scientific experience" (sometimes referred to as "know-how") has the meaning ascribed to it in paragraph 11 *et seq.* of the Commentary to Article 12 of the OECD Model. Consistent with that meaning, the term may include information that is ancillary to a right otherwise giving rise to royalties, such as a patent or secret process.

Know-how also may include, in limited cases, technical information that is conveyed through technical or consultancy services. It does not include general educational training of the user's employees, nor does it include information developed especially for the user, such as a technical plan or design developed according to the user's specifications. Thus, as provided in paragraph 11.3 of the Commentary to Article 12 of the OECD Model, the term "royalties" does not include payments received as consideration for after-sales service, for services rendered by a seller to a purchaser under a warranty, or for pure technical assistance.

The term "royalties" also does not include payments for professional services (such as

45

architectural, engineering, legal, managerial, medical or software development services). For example, income from the design of a refinery by an engineer (even if the engineer employed know-how in the process of rendering the design) or the production of a legal brief by a lawyer is not income from the transfer of know-how taxable under Article 13, but is income from services taxable under either Article 7 (Business Profits) or Article 15 (Income from Employment) as applicable. Professional services may be embodied in property that gives rise to royalties, however. Thus, if a professional contracts to develop patentable property and retains rights in the resulting property under the development contract, subsequent license payments made for those rights would be royalties.

*Paragraph 4*

This paragraph provides an exception to paragraphs 1 and 2 in cases where the beneficial owner of the royalties carries on business through a permanent establishment in the state of source and the right or property in respect of which the royalties are paid is effectively connected with such permanent establishment. In such cases the provisions of Article 7 (Business Profits) will apply.

In the case of a permanent establishment that once existed in a Contracting State but that no longer exists, the provisions of this paragraph also apply, by virtue of paragraph 5 of Article 7 (Business Profits) to royalties paid with respect to rights or property that would be effectively connected to such permanent establishment if it did exist in the year of payment or accrual. Accordingly, such royalties would remain taxable under the provisions of Article 7, and not under this Article.

*Paragraph 5*

Paragraph 5 contains the source rule for royalties. Under paragraph 5, royalties are treated as arising in a Contracting State only to the extent that they are in consideration for the use of, or the right to use, property, information or experience in that State. This source rule parallels the source rule in Code section 861(a)(4).

*Paragraph 6*

Paragraph 6 provides that in cases involving special relationships between the payer and beneficial owner of royalties, Article 13 applies only to the extent the royalties would have been paid absent such special relationships (*i.e.*, an arm's-length royalty). Any excess amount of royalties paid remains taxable according to the laws of the two Contracting States, with due regard to the other provisions of the Convention. If, for example, the excess amount is treated as a distribution of corporate profits under domestic law, such excess amount will be taxed as a dividend rather than as royalties, but the tax imposed on the dividend payment will be subject to the rate limitations of paragraph 2 of Article 10 (Dividends).

*Relationship to Other Articles*

Notwithstanding the foregoing limitations on source country taxation of royalties, the saving clause of paragraph 4 of Article 1 (General Scope) permits the United States to tax its residents and citizens, subject to the special foreign tax credit rules of paragraph 4 of Article 23 (Relief from Double Taxation), as if the Convention had not come into force.

As with other benefits of the Convention, the benefits of exclusive residence State taxation of royalties under paragraph 1 of Article 13 are available to a resident of the other State only if that resident is entitled to those benefits under Article 22 (Limitation on Benefits).

## ARTICLE 14 (CAPITAL GAINS)

Article 14 assigns either primary or exclusive taxing jurisdiction over gains from the alienation of property to the State of residence or the State of source.

*Paragraph 1*

Paragraph 1 of Article 14 preserves the non-exclusive right of the State of source to tax gains from the alienation of real property situated in that State

*Paragraph 2*

Paragraph 2 allows the United States to tax in accordance with Code section 897 gains derived by a resident of Poland that are attributable to the alienation of a United States real property interest. Under Code section 897(c) the term "United States real property interest" includes shares in a U.S. corporation that owns sufficient U.S. real property interests to satisfy an asset-ratio test on certain testing dates. The term also includes certain foreign corporations that have elected to be treated as U.S. corporations for this purpose. *See* Code section 897(i). In addition, any distribution made by a REIT or certain RICs is taxable under paragraph 1 of Article 14 (rather than under Article 10 (Dividends)) to the extent that it is attributable to gains derived from the alienation of U.S. real property interests. *See* Code section 897(h).

*Paragraph 3*

Paragraph 3 permits Poland to tax gains derived by a resident of the United States from the alienation of two categories of property. The first category is described in subparagraph 3(a) as shares, including rights to acquire shares, deriving more than 50 percent of their value directly or indirectly from real property situated in Poland. The second category is described in subparagraph 3(b) as an interest in a partnership or trust to the extent that the assets of the partnership or trust consist in aggregate more than 50 percent of real property situated in Poland or of shares referred to in subparagraph 3(a).

*Paragraph 4*

Paragraph 4 deals with the taxation of certain gains from the alienation of movable property forming part of the business property of a permanent establishment that an enterprise of a Contracting State has in the other Contracting State. This also includes gains from the alien-ation of such a permanent establishment (alone or with the whole enterprise). Such gains may be

47

taxed in the State in which the permanent establishment is located.

A resident of Poland that is a partner in a partnership doing business in the United States generally will have a permanent establishment in the United States as a result of the activities of the partnership, assuming that the activities of the partnership rise to the level of a permanent establishment. *See* Rev. Rul. 91-32, 1991-1 C.B. 107. Further, under paragraph 4, the United States generally may tax a partner's distributive share of income realized by a partnership on the disposition of movable property forming part of the business property of the partnership in the United States.

Paragraph 5 of Article 7 (Business Profits) provides that gains subject to paragraph 4 may be taxed in the State in which the permanent establishment is located, regardless of whether the permanent establishment exists at the time of the alienation. This rule incorporates the rule of Code section 864(c)(6). Accordingly, income that is attributable to a permanent establishment, but that is deferred and received after the permanent establishment no longer exists, may nevertheless be taxed by the State in which the permanent establishment was located.

*Paragraph 5*

This paragraph limits the taxing jurisdiction of the State of source with respect to gains from the alienation of ships or aircraft operated in international traffic by the enterprise alienating the ship or aircraft and from property (other than real property) pertaining to the operation or use of such ships or aircraft.

Under paragraph 5, such gains are taxable only in the Contracting State in which the alienator is resident. Notwithstanding paragraph 4, the rules of this paragraph apply even if the income is attributable to a permanent establishment maintained by the enterprise in the other Contracting State. This result is consistent with the allocation of taxing rights under Article 8 (Shipping and Air Transport).

*Paragraph 6*

Paragraph 6 provides a rule similar to paragraph 5 with respect to gains from the alienation of containers and related personal property. Such gains derived by a enterprise of a Contracting State shall be taxable only in that Contracting State unless the containers were used for the transport of goods or merchandise solely within the other Contracting State. The other Contracting State may not tax even if the gain is attributable to a permanent establishment maintained by the enterprise in that other Contracting State.

*Paragraph 7*

Paragraph 6 grants to the State of residence of the alienator the exclusive right to tax gains from the alienation of property other than property referred to in paragraphs 1 through 6. For example, gain derived from the alienation of shares, other than shares described in paragraphs 2 or 3, debt instruments and various financial instruments, may be taxed only in the State of residence, to the extent such income is not otherwise characterized as income taxable under another article (*e.g.*, Article 10 (Dividends) or Article 11 (Interest)). Similarly gain derived from the alienation of tangible personal property, other than tangible personal property described in paragraph 3, may be taxed only in the State of residence of the alienator.

Gain derived from the alienation of any property, such as a patent or copyright, that produces income covered by Article 13 (Royalties) is governed by the rules of Article 13 and not by this article, provided that such gain is of the type described in paragraph 3(b) of Article 13 (*i.e.*, it is contingent on the productivity, use, or disposition of the property).

Gains derived by a resident of a Contracting State from real property located in a third state are not taxable in the other Contracting State, even if the sale is attributable to a permanent establishment located in the other Contracting State.

*Relationship to Other Articles*

Notwithstanding the foregoing limitations on taxation of certain gains by the State of source, the saving clause of paragraph 4 of Article 1 (General Scope) permits the United States to tax its citizens and residents as if the Convention had not come into effect. Thus, any limitation in this Article on the right of the United States to tax gains does not apply to gains of a U.S. citizen or resident.

The benefits of this Article are also subject to the provisions of Article 22 (Limitation on Benefits). Thus, only a resident of a Contracting State that satisfies one of the conditions in Article 22 is entitled to the benefits of this Article.

Paragraph 5 of Article 23 (Relief from Double Taxation) coordinates the tax systems of the Contracting States to avoid double taxation that could result from the imposition of exit tax regimes on individuals who relinquish citizenship or long-term residence status.


## ARTICLE 15 (INCOME FROM EMPLOYMENT)

Article 15 apportions taxing jurisdiction over remuneration derived by a resident of a Contracting State as an employee between the States of source and residence.

*Paragraph 1*

The general rule of Article 15 is contained in paragraph 1. Article 15 applies to any form of compensation for employment, including payments in kind. Remuneration derived by a resident of a Contracting State as an employee may be taxed by the State of residence, and the remuneration also may be taxed by the other Contracting State to the extent derived from employment exercised (*i.e.*, services performed) in that other Contracting State. Paragraph 1 also provides that the more specific rules of Articles 16 (Directors' Fees), 18 (Pensions, Social Security, Annuities, Alimony and Child Support), and 19 (Government Service) apply in the case of employment income described in one of those Articles. Thus, even though the State of source has a right to tax employment income under Article 15, it may not have the right to tax that income under the Convention if the income is described, for example, in Article 18 (Pensions, Social Security, Annuities, Alimony and Child Support) and is not taxable in the State of source under the provisions of that Article.

Article 15 applies regardless of the timing of actual payment for services. Consequently, a person who receives the right to a future payment in consideration for services rendered in a Contracting State would be taxable in that State even if the payment is received at a time when the recipient is a resident of the other Contracting State. Thus, a bonus paid to a resident of a Contracting State with respect to services performed in the other Contracting State with respect to a particular taxable year would be subject to Article 15 for that year even if it was paid after the close of the year. An annuity received for services performed in a taxable year could be subject to Article 15 despite the fact that it was paid in subsequent years. In that case, it would be necessary to determine whether the payment constitutes deferred compensation, taxable under Article 15, or a qualified pension subject to the rules of Article 18. Article 15 also applies to income derived from the exercise of stock options granted with respect to services performed in the host State, even if those stock options are exercised after the employee has left the host State. If Article 15 is found to apply, whether such payments were taxable in the State where the employment was exercised would depend on whether the tests of paragraph 2 were satisfied in the year in which the services to which the payment relates were performed.

*Paragraph 2*

Paragraph 2 sets forth an exception to the general rule that employment income may be taxed in the State where it is exercised. Under paragraph 2, the State where the employment is exercised may not tax the income from the employment if three conditions are satisfied: (a) the individual is present in the other Contracting State for a period or periods not exceeding 183 days in any 12-month period that begins or ends during the relevant taxable year (*i.e.*, in the United States, the calendar year in which the services are performed); (b) the remuneration is paid by, or on behalf of, an employer who is not a resident of that other Contracting State; and (c) the remuneration is not borne as a deductible expense by a permanent establishment that the employer has in that other State. In order for the remuneration to be exempt from tax in the source State, all three conditions must be satisfied. This exception is identical to that set forth in the OECD Model.

The 183-day period in subparagraph 2(a) is to be measured using the "days of physical presence" method. Under this method, the days that are counted include any day in which a part of the day is spent in the host country. (*See* Rev. Rul. 56-24, 1956-1 C.B. 851.) Thus, days that are counted include the days of arrival and departure; weekends and holidays on which the employee does not work but is present within the country; vacation days spent in the country before, during or after the employment period, unless the individual's presence before or after the employment can be shown to be independent of his presence there for employment purposes; and time during periods of sickness, training periods, strikes, etc., when the individual is present but not working. If illness prevented the individual from leaving the country in sufficient time to qualify for the benefit, those days will not count. Also, any part of a day spent in the host country while in transit between two points outside the host country is not counted. If the individual is a resident of the host country for part of the taxable year concerned and a nonresident for the remainder of the year, the individual's days of presence as a resident do not count for purposes of determining whether the 183-day period is exceeded.

Subparagraphs 2(b) and 2(c) are intended to ensure that a Contracting State will not be required to allow a deduction to the payor for compensation paid and at the same time to exempt the employee on the amount received. Accordingly, if a foreign person pays the salary of an employee who is employed in the host State, but a host State corporation or permanent establishment reimburses the payor with a payment that can be identified as a reimbursement, neither subparagraph 2(b) nor 2(c), as the case may be, will be considered to have been fulfilled.

The reference to remuneration "borne by" a permanent establishment is understood to encompass all expenses that economically are incurred and not merely expenses that are currently deductible for tax purposes. Accordingly, the expenses referred to include expenses that are capitalizable as well as those that are currently deductible. Further, salaries paid by residents that are exempt from income taxation may be considered to be borne by a permanent establishment notwithstanding the fact that the expenses will be neither deductible nor capitalizable since the payor is exempt from tax.

For the purpose of determining the profits attributable to a permanent establishment pursuant to paragraph 2 of Article 7 (Business Profits), the remuneration paid to an employee of an enterprise of a Contracting State for employment services rendered in the other State for the benefit of the permanent establishment of the enterprise situated in that other State may, given the circumstances, either give rise to a direct deduction or give rise to the deduction of a notional charge, *e.g.*, for services rendered to the permanent establishment by another part of the enterprise. In the latter case, since the notional charge required by the legal fiction of the separate and independent enterprise that is applicable under paragraph 2 of Article 7 is merely a mechanism provided for by that paragraph for the sole purpose of determining the profits attributable to the permanent establishment, this fiction does not affect the determination of whether or not the remuneration is borne by the permanent establishment.

*Paragraph 3*

Paragraph 3 contains a special rule applicable to remuneration for services performed by a resident of a Contracting State as an employee aboard a ship or aircraft operated in international traffic. Such remuneration may be taxed only in the State of residence of the employee if the services are performed as a member of the regular complement of the ship or aircraft. The "regular complement" includes the crew. In the case of a cruise ship, for example, it may also include others, such as entertainers, lecturers, etc., employed by the shipping company to serve on the ship throughout its voyage. The use of the term "regular complement" is intended to clarify that a person who exercises his employment as, for example, an insurance salesman while aboard a ship or aircraft is not covered by this paragraph.

If a U.S. citizen who is resident in Poland performs services as an employee in the United States and meets the conditions of paragraph 2 for source country exemption, he nevertheless is taxable in the United States by virtue of the saving clause of paragraph 4 of Article 1 (General Scope), subject to the special foreign tax credit rule of paragraph 4 of Article 23 (Relief from

51

Double Taxation).

## ARTICLE 16 (DIRECTORS' FEES)

This Article provides that a Contracting State may tax the fees and other compensation paid by a company that is a resident of that State to an individual resident of the other Contracting State in his capacity as a director of the company. This rule is an exception to the more general rules of Articles 7 (Business Profits) and 15 (Income from Employment). Thus, for example, in determining whether a director's fee paid to a non-employee director is subject to tax in the country of residence of the corporation, it is not relevant to establish whether the fee is attributable to a permanent establishment in that State.

*Relationship with other Articles*

This Article is subject to the saving clause of paragraph 4 of Article 1 (General Scope).

## ARTICLE 17 (ENTERTAINERS AND SPORTSMEN)

This Article deals with the taxation in a Contracting State of entertainers and sportsmen resident in the other Contracting State from the performance of their services as such. The Article applies both to the income of an entertainer or sportsman who performs services on his own behalf and one who performs services on behalf of another person, either as an employee of that person, or pursuant to any other arrangement. The rules of this Article take precedence, in some circumstances, over those of Articles 7 (Business Profits) and 15 (Income from Employment).

This Article applies only with respect to the income of entertainers and sportsmen. Others involved in a performance or athletic event, such as producers, directors, technicians, managers, coaches, etc., remain subject to the provisions of Articles 7 and 15. In addition, except as provided in paragraph 2, income earned by juridical persons is not covered by Article 17.

*Paragraph 1*

Paragraph 1 describes the circumstances in which a Contracting State may tax the performance income of an entertainer or sportsman who is a resident of the other Contracting State. Under the paragraph, income derived by an individual resident of a Contracting State from activities as an entertainer or sportsman exercised in the other Contracting State may be taxed in that other State if the amount of the gross receipts derived by the performer exceeds $20,000 (or its equivalent in Polish legal tender) for the taxable year. The $20,000 includes expenses reimbursed to the individual or borne on his behalf. If the gross receipts exceed $20,000, the full amount, not just the excess, may be taxed in the State of performance.

The OECD Model provides for taxation by the country of performance of the remuneration of entertainers or sportsmen with no dollar or time threshold. This Convention introduces the monetary threshold to distinguish between two groups of entertainers and athletes –those who are paid relatively large sums of money for very short periods of service, and who would, therefore, normally be exempt from host country tax under the standard personal services income rules, and those who earn relatively modest amounts and are, therefore, not easily distinguishable from those who earn other types of personal service income. The United States has entered a reservation to the OECD Model on this point.

Tax may be imposed under paragraph 1 even if the performer would have been exempt from tax under Article 7 (Business Profits) or Article 15 (Income from Employment). On the other hand if the performer would be exempt from host-country tax under Article 17, but would be taxable under either Article 7 or Article 15, tax may be imposed under either of those Articles. Thus, for example, if a performer derives remuneration from his activities in an independent capacity, and the performer does not have a permanent establishment in the host State, he may be taxed by the host State in accordance with Article 17 if his remuneration exceeds $20,000 annually, despite the fact that he generally would be exempt from host State taxation under Article 7. However, a performer who receives less than the $20,000 threshold amount and therefore is not taxable under Article 17 nevertheless may be subject to tax in the host country under Article 7 or Article 15 if the tests for host-country taxability under the relevant Article are met. For example, if an entertainer who is an independent contractor earns $14,000 of income in a State for the calendar year, but the income is attributable to his permanent establishment in the State of performance, that State may tax his income under Article 7.

Since it frequently is not possible to know until year-end whether the income an entertainer or sportsman derived from performances in a Contracting State will exceed $20,000, nothing in the Convention precludes that Contracting State from withholding tax during the year and refunding it after the close of the year if the taxability threshold has not been met.

As explained in paragraph 9 of the Commentary to Article 17 of the OECD Model, Article 17 of the Convention applies to all income connected with a performance by the entertainer, such as appearance fees, award or prize money, and a share of the gate receipts. Income derived from a Contracting State by a performer who is a resident of the other Contracting State from other than actual performance, such as royalties from record sales and payments for product endorsements, is not covered by this Article, but by other articles of the Convention, such as Article 13 (Royalties) or Article 7. For example, if an entertainer receives royalty income from the sale of live recordings, the royalty income would be exempt from source State tax under Article 12, even if the performance was conducted in the source country, although the entertainer could be taxed in the source country with respect to income from the performance itself under Article 17 if the dollar threshold is exceeded.

In determining whether income falls under Article 17 or another Article, the controlling factor will be whether the income in question is predominantly attributable to the performance itself or to other activities or property rights. For instance, a fee paid to a performer for endorsement of a performance in which the performer will participate would be considered to be so closely associated with the performance itself that it normally would fall within Article 17. Similarly, a sponsorship fee paid by a business in return for the right to attach its name to the performance would be so closely associated with the performance that it would fall under Article 17 as well. As indicated in paragraph 9 of the Commentary to Article 17 of the OECD Model, however, a cancellation fee would not be considered to fall within Article 16 but would be dealt with under Article 7 or15.

As indicated in paragraph 4 of the Commentary to Article 17 of the OECD Model, where an individual fulfills a dual role as performer and non-performer (such as a player-coach or an actor-director), but his role in one of the two capacities is negligible, the predominant character of the individual's activities should control the characterization of those activities. In other cases there should be an apportionment between the performance-related compensation and other compensation.

Consistent with Article 15, Article 17 also applies regardless of the timing of actual payment for services. Thus, a bonus paid to a resident of a Contracting State with respect to a performance in the other Contracting State during a particular taxable year would be subject to Article 17 for that year even if it was paid after the close of the year. The determination as to whether the $20,000 threshold has been exceeded is determined separately with respect to each year of payment. Accordingly, if an actor who is a resident of one Contracting State receives residual payments over time with respect to a movie that was filmed in the other Contracting State, the payments do not have to be aggregated from one year to another to determine whether the total payments have finally exceeded $20,000. Otherwise, residual payments received many years later could retroactively subject all earlier payments to tax by the other Contracting State.

*Paragraph 2*

Paragraph 2 is intended to address the potential for circumvention of the rule in paragraph 1 when a performer's income does not accrue directly to the performer himself, but to another person. Foreign performers frequently perform in the United States as employees of, or under contract with, a company or other person.

The relationship may truly be one of employee and employer, with no circumvention of paragraph 1 either intended or realized. On the other hand, the "employer" may, for example, be a company established and owned by the performer, which is merely acting as the nominal income recipient in respect of the remuneration for the performance (a "star company"). The performer may act as an "employee," receive a modest salary, and arrange to receive the remainder of the income from his performance from the company in another form or at a later time. In such case, absent the provisions of paragraph 2, the income arguably could escape host-country tax because the company earns business profits but has no permanent establishment in that country. The performer may largely or entirely escape host-country tax by receiving only a small salary, perhaps small enough to place him below the dollar threshold in paragraph 1. The performer might arrange to receive further payments in a later year, when he is not subject to host-country tax, perhaps as dividends or liquidating distributions.

Paragraph 2 seeks to prevent this type of abuse while at the same time protecting the taxpayers' rights to the benefits of the Convention when there is a legitimate employee-employer relationship between the performer and the person providing his services. Under paragraph 2, when the income accrues to a person other than the performer, the income may be taxed in the Contracting State where the performer's services are exercised, without regard to the provisions of Article 7 or Article 15, unless the contract pursuant to which the personal activities are performed allows such other person other than the performer to designate the individual who is to perform the personal activities. This rule is based on the U.S. domestic law provision characterizing income from certain personal service contracts as foreign personal holding company income in the context of the foreign personal holding company provisions. *See* Code section 954(c)(1)(I). The premise of this rule is that, in a case where a performer is using another person in an attempt to circumvent the provisions of paragraph 1, the recipient of the services of the performer would contract with a person other than that performer (*i.e.*, a company employing the performer) only if the recipient of the services were certain that the performer himself would perform the services. If instead the person is allowed to designate the individual who is to perform the services, then likely the person is a service company not formed to circumvent the provisions of paragraph 1. The following example illustrates the operation of this rule.

Example. Company O, a resident of Poland, is engaged in the business of operating an orchestra. Company O enters into a contract with Company A pursuant to which Company O agrees to carry out two performances in the United States in consideration of which Company A will pay Company O $200,000. The contract designates two individuals, a conductor and a flutist, that must perform as part of the orchestra, and allows Company O to designate the other members of the orchestra. Because the contract does not give Company O any discretion to determine whether the conductor or the flutist perform personal services under the contract, the portion of the $200,000 which is attributable to the personal services of the conductor and the flutist may be taxed by the United States pursuant to paragraph 2. The remaining portion of the $200,000, which is attributable to the personal services of performers that Company O may designate, is not subject to tax by the United States pursuant to paragraph 2.

In cases where paragraph 2 is applicable, the income of the "employer" may be subject to tax in the host Contracting State even if it has no permanent establishment in the host country. Taxation under paragraph 2 is on the person providing the services of the performer. This paragraph does not affect the rules of paragraph 1, which apply to the performer himself. The income taxable by virtue of paragraph 2 is reduced to the extent of salary payments to the performer, which fall under paragraph 1.

For purposes of paragraph 2, income is deemed to accrue to another person (*i.e.*, the person providing the services of the performer) if that other person has control over, or the right to receive, gross income in respect of the services of the performer.

Since pursuant to Article 1 (General Scope) the Convention only applies to persons who are residents of one of the Contracting States, income of the star company would not be eligible for benefits of the Convention if the company is not a resident of one of the Contracting States.

*Relationship to other Articles*

This Article is subject to the provisions of the saving clause of paragraph 4 of Article 1 (General Scope). Thus, if an entertainer or a sportsman who is resident in Poland is a citizen of the United States, the United States may tax all of his income from performances in the United States without regard to the provisions of this Article, subject, however, to the special foreign tax credit provisions of paragraph 4 of Article 23 (Relief from Double Taxation). In addition, benefits of this Article are subject to the provisions of Article 22 (Limitation on Benefits).

## ARTICLE 18 (PENSIONS, SOCIAL SECURITY, ANNUITIES, ALIMONY, AND CHILD SUPPORT)

This Article deals with the taxation of private (i.e., non-government service) pensions and annuities, social security benefits, alimony and child support payments.

*Paragraph 1*

Paragraph 1 provides that distributions from pensions, annuities and other similar payments beneficially owned by a resident of a Contracting State in consideration of past employment are taxable only in the State of residence of the beneficiary. The terms "pensions" and "other similar payments" include both periodic and single sum payments.

The terms "pensions" and "other similar payments" are intended to encompass payments made by qualified private retirement plans. In the United States, the plans encompassed by paragraph 1 include: qualified plans under section 401(a), individual retirement plans (including individual retirement plans that are part of a simplified employee pension plan that satisfies section 408(k), individual retirement accounts and section 408(p) accounts), section 403(a) qualified annuity plans, and section 403(b) plans. Distributions from section 457 plans may also fall under paragraph 1 if they are not paid with respect to government services covered by Article 19 (Government Service).

Pensions in respect of government services covered by Article 19 are not covered by this paragraph. They are covered either by paragraph 2 of this Article if they are in the form of social security benefits, or by paragraph 2 of Article 19. Thus, Article 19 generally covers section 457(g), 401(a), 403(a) and 403(b) plans established for government employees, including the Thrift Savings Plan (section 7701(j)).

*Paragraph 2*

Paragraph 2 contains an exception to the residence State's right to tax pensions and other similar remuneration under paragraph 1. Under paragraph 2, the State of residence must exempt from tax any amount of such pensions or other similar remuneration that would be exempt from tax in the Contracting State in which the pension fund is established if the recipient were a resident of that State. Thus, for example, a distribution from a U.S. "Roth IRA" to a resident of Poland would be exempt from tax in Poland to the same extent the distribution would be exempt from tax in the United States if it were distributed to a U.S. resident. The same is true with respect to distributions from a traditional IRA to the extent that the distribution represents a return of non-deductible contributions. Similarly, if the distribution were not subject to tax when it was "rolled over" into another U.S. IRA (but not, for example, to a pension fund in the other Contracting State), then the distribution would be exempt from tax in Poland.

*Paragraph 3*

The treatment of social security benefits is dealt with in paragraph 3. This paragraph provides that, notwithstanding the provision of paragraph 1 under which private pensions are taxable exclusively in the State of residence of the beneficial owner, payments made by one of the Contracting States under the provisions of its social security or similar legislation to a resident of the other Contracting State or to a citizen of the United States will be taxable only in the Contracting State making the payment. The reference to U.S. citizens is necessary to ensure that a social security payment by Poland to a U.S. citizen who is not resident in the United States will not be taxable by the United States.

This paragraph applies to social security beneficiaries whether they have contributed to the system as private sector or Government employees. The phrase "similar legislation" is intended to refer to United States tier 1 Railroad Retirement benefits.

*Paragraph 4*

Paragraph 4 provides that, if a resident of a Contracting State participates in a pension fund established in the other Contracting State, the State of residence will not tax the income of the pension fund with respect to that resident until a distribution is made from the pension fund. Thus, for example, if a U.S. citizen contributes to a U.S. qualified plan while working in the United States and then establishes residence in Poland, paragraph 1 prevents Poland from taxing currently the plan's earnings and accretions with respect to that individual. When the resident receives a distribution from the pension fund, that distribution may be subject to tax in Poland, the State of residence, under paragraph 1 of Article 18. Paragraph 4 also provides that a transfer from a pension fund located in a Contracting State to another pension fund located in that same State shall not be taxed by either Contracting State.

*Paragraph 5*

Paragraph 5 provides that alimony and periodic payments for the support of a child made pursuant to a written agreement or a decree of divorce, separate maintenance, or compulsory support paid by a resident of a Contracting State to a resident of the other Contracting State shall be exempt from tax in both Contracting States. The term "alimony" as used in this paragraph means periodic payments made pursuant to a written separation agreement or a decree of divorce, separate maintenance or compulsory support which are taxable to the recipient under the laws of the State of which he is a resident.

*Relationship to other Articles*

Paragraphs 1 and 4 of Article 18 are subject to the saving clause of paragraph 4 of Article 1 (General Scope). Thus, a U.S. citizen who is resident in Poland, and receives a pension distribution from the United States, may be subject to U.S. tax on the payment, notwithstanding the rules in the paragraphs that give the State of residence of the recipient the exclusive taxing right. Paragraphs 2, 3 and 5 are excepted from the saving clause by virtue of subparagraph 5(a) of Article 1. Thus, the United States will not tax U.S. citizens and residents on the income described in those paragraphs even if such amounts otherwise would be subject to tax under U.S. law.

## ARTICLE 19 (GOVERNMENT SERVICE)

*Paragraph 1*

Subparagraphs 1(a) and 1(b) deal with the taxation of government compensation (other than a pension addressed in paragraph 2). Subparagraph 1(a) provides that remuneration paid to any individual who is rendering services to that State, political subdivision or local authority is exempt from tax by the other State. Under subparagraph 1(b), such payments are, however, taxable exclusively in the other State (*i.e.*, the host State) if the services are rendered in that other State and the individual is a resident of that State who is either a national of that State or a person who did not become resident of that State solely for purposes of rendering the services. The paragraph applies to anyone performing services for a government, whether as a government employee, an independent contractor, or an employee of an independent contractor.

*Paragraph 2*

Paragraph 2 deals with the taxation of pensions paid by, or out of funds created by, one of the States, or a political subdivision or a local authority thereof, to an individual in respect of services rendered to that State or subdivision or authority. Subparagraph 2(a) provides that such pensions are taxable only in that State. Subparagraph 2(b) provides an exception under which such pensions are taxable only in the other State if the individual is a resident of, and a national of, that other State.

Pensions paid to retired civilian and military employees of a Government of either State are intended to be covered under paragraph 2. When benefits paid by a State in respect of services rendered to that State or a subdivision or authority are in the form of social security benefits, however, those payments are covered by paragraph 3 of Article 18 (Pensions, Social Security, Annuities, Alimony, and Child Support). As a general matter, the result will be the same whether Article 18 or Article 19 applies, since social security benefits are taxable exclusively by the source country and so are government pensions. The result will differ only when the payment is made to a citizen and resident of the other Contracting State, who is not also a citizen of the paying State. In such a case, social security benefits continue to be taxable at source while government pensions become taxable only in the residence country.

*Paragraph 3*

Paragraph 3 provides that the remuneration described in paragraph 1 will be subject to the rules of Articles 15 (Income from Employment), 16 (Directors' Fees), 17 (Entertainers and Sportsmen) or 18 (Pensions, Social Security, Annuities, Alimony, and Child Support) if the recipient of the income is employed by a business conducted by a government.

*Relationship to other Articles*

Under paragraph 5(b) of Article 1 (General Scope), the saving clause (paragraph 4 of Article 1) does not apply to the benefits conferred by one of the States under Article 19 if the recipient of the benefits is neither a citizen of that State, nor a person who has been admitted for permanent residence there (*i.e.*, in the United States, a "green card" holder). Thus, a resident of a Contracting State who in the course of performing functions of a governmental nature becomes a resident of the other State (but not a permanent resident), would be entitled to the benefits of this Article. However, an individual who receives a pension paid by the Government of Poland in respect of services rendered to the Government of Poland shall be taxable on this pension only in Poland unless the individual is a U.S. citizen or acquires a U.S. green card.

## ARTICLE 20 (STUDENTS AND TRAINEES)

This Article provides rules for host-country taxation of visiting students (including pupils) and business trainees. Persons who meet the tests of the Article will be exempt from tax in the State that they are visiting with respect to designated classes of income. Several conditions must be satisfied in order for an individual to be entitled to the benefits of this Article.

First, the visitor must have been, either at the time of his arrival in the host State or immediately before, a resident of the other Contracting State.

Second, the primary purpose of the visit must be the education or training of the visitor. Thus, if the visitor comes principally to work in the host State but also is a part-time student, he would not be entitled to the benefits of this Article, even with respect to any payments he may receive from abroad for his maintenance or education, and regardless of whether or not he is in a degree program. If the student is engaged in full time study, the primary purpose of his visit to the host State will be deemed to have as its primary purpose education. Whether a student is to be considered full-time will be determined by the rules of the educational institution at which he is studying.

*Paragraph 1*

The host-country exemption in paragraph 1 applies to payments received by the student (including a pupil) or business trainee for the purpose of his maintenance, education or training that arise outside the host State. A payment will be considered to arise outside the host State if the payer is located outside the host State. Thus, if an employer from one of the Contracting States sends an employee to the other Contracting State for training, the payments the trainee receives from abroad from his employer for his maintenance or training while he is present in the host State will be exempt from tax in the host State. Where appropriate, substance prevails over form in determining the identity of the payer. Thus, for example, payments made directly or indirectly by a U.S. person with whom the visitor is training, but which have been routed through a source outside the United States (*e.g.*, a foreign subsidiary), are not treated as arising outside the United States for this purpose.

In the case of a business trainee, the benefits of paragraph 1 will extend only for a period of one year from the time that the visitor first arrives in the host country. If, however, a trainee remains in the host country for a second year, thus losing the benefits of paragraph 1, he would not retroactively lose the benefits of the paragraph for the first year.

*Paragraph 2*

Paragraph 2 provides a limited exemption for remuneration from personal services rendered in the host State up to $9,000 United States dollars (or its equivalent in Polish legal tender) per taxable year. The specified amount is intended to equalize the position of a U.S. resident who is entitled to the standard deduction and the personal exemption with that of a student who files as a non-resident alien and therefore is not entitled to such statutory benefits.

*Paragraph 3*

The term "business trainee" is defined as a person who is in the host State temporarily for the purpose of securing training that is necessary to qualify to pursue a profession or professional specialty. Moreover, the person must be employed or under contract with a resident of the other Contracting State and must be receiving the training from someone who is not related to its employer. Thus, a business trainee might include a lawyer employed by a law firm in one Contracting State who works for one year as a *stagiaire* in an unrelated law firm in the other Contracting State. However, the term would not include a manager who normally is employed by a parent company in one Contracting State who is sent to the other Contracting State to run a factory owned by a subsidiary of the parent company.

*Relationship to other Articles*

The saving clause of paragraph 4 of Article 1 (General Scope) does not apply to this Article with respect to an individual who is neither a citizen of the host State nor has been admitted for permanent residence there. The saving clause, however, does apply with respect to citizens and permanent residents of the host State. Thus, a U.S. citizen who is a resident of Poland and who visits the United States as a full-time student at an accredited university will not be exempt from U.S. tax on remittances from abroad that otherwise constitute U.S. taxable income. A person, however, who is not a U.S. citizen, and who visits the United States as a student and remains long enough to become a resident under U.S. law, but does not become a permanent resident (*i.e.*, does not acquire a green card), will be entitled to the full benefits of the Article.

## ARTICLE 21 (OTHER INCOME)

Article 21 generally assigns taxing jurisdiction over income not dealt with in the other Articles (Articles 6 (Income from Real Property) through Article 20 (Students and Trainees)) of the Convention to the State of residence of the beneficial owner of the income. In order for an item of income to be "dealt with" in another article it must be the type of income described in the article and, in most cases, it must have its source in a Contracting State. For example, all royalty income that arises in a Contracting State and that is beneficially owned by a resident of the other Contracting State is "dealt with" in Article 13 (Royalties). However, profits derived in the conduct of a business are "dealt with" in Article 7 (Business Profits) whether or not they have their source in one of the Contracting States.

Examples of items of income covered by Article 21 include income from gambling, punitive (but not compensatory) damages and covenants not to compete. Article 21 would also apply to income from a variety of financial transactions, where such income does not arise in the course of the conduct of a trade or business. For example, income from notional principal contracts and other derivatives would fall within Article 21 if derived by persons not engaged in the trade or business of dealing in such instruments, unless such instruments were being used to hedge risks arising in a trade or business. It would also apply to securities lending fees derived by an institutional investor. Further, in most cases guarantee fees paid within an intercompany group would be covered by Article 21, unless the guarantor were engaged in the business of providing such guarantees to unrelated parties.

Article 21 also applies to items of income that are not "dealt with" in the other articles because of their source or some other characteristic. For example, Article 11 (Interest) addresses only the taxation of interest arising in a Contracting State. Interest arising in a third State that is not attributable to a permanent establishment, therefore, is subject to Article 21.

Distributions from partnerships are not generally "dealt with" under Article 21 because partnership distributions generally do not constitute income. Under the Code, partners include in income their distributive share of partnership income annually, and partnership distributions themselves generally do not give rise to income. This would also be the case under U.S. law with respect to distributions from trusts. Trust income and distributions that, under the Code, have the character of the associated distributable net income would generally be covered by another article of the Convention. *See* Code section 641 et seq.

*Paragraph 1*

The general rule of Article 21 is contained in paragraph 1. Items of income not dealt with in other articles and beneficially owned by a resident of a Contracting State will be taxable only in the State of residence. This exclusive right of taxation applies whether or not the residence State exercises its right to tax the income covered by the Article.

The reference in this paragraph to "items of income beneficially owned by a resident of a Contracting State" rather than simply "items of income of a resident of a Contracting State," as in the OECD Model, is intended merely to make explicit the understanding in other treaties that the exclusive residence taxation provided by paragraph 1 applies only when a resident of a Contracting State is the beneficial owner of the income. Thus, source taxation of income not dealt with in other articles of the Convention is not limited by paragraph 1 if it is nominally paid to a resident of the other Contracting State, but is beneficially owned by a resident of a third State. However, income received by a nominee on behalf of a resident of that other State would be entitled to benefits.

The term "beneficially owned" is not defined in the Convention, and is, therefore, defined as under the internal law of the country imposing tax (*i.e.*, the source country). The person who beneficially owns the income for purposes of Article 21 is the person to which the income is attributable for tax purposes under the laws of the source State.

*Paragraph 2*

61

This paragraph provides an exception to the general rule of paragraph 1 for income from a right or property that is effectively connected to a permanent establishment maintained in a Contracting State by a resident of the other Contracting State. The taxation of such income is governed by the provisions of Article 7 (Business Profits). Therefore, income arising outside the United States from a right or property that is effectively connected to a permanent establishment maintained in the United States by a resident of the other Contracting State generally would be taxable by the United States under the provisions of Article 7. This would be true even if the income is sourced in a third State.

*Relationship to Other Articles*

This Article is subject to the saving clause of paragraph 4 of Article 1 (General Scope). Thus, the United States may tax the income of a resident of Poland that is not dealt with elsewhere in the Convention, if that resident is a citizen of the United States. The Article is also subject to the provisions of Article 22 (Limitation on Benefits). Thus, if a resident of Poland earns income that falls within the scope of paragraph 1 of Article 21, but that is taxable by the United States under U.S. law, the income would be exempt from U.S. tax under the provisions of Article 21 only if the resident satisfies one of the tests of Article 22 for entitlement to benefits.

## ARTICLE 22 (LIMITATION ON BENEFITS)

Article 22 contains anti-treaty-shopping provisions that are intended to prevent residents of third countries from benefiting from what is intended to be a reciprocal agreement between two countries. In general, the provision does not rely on a determination of purpose or intention but instead sets forth a series of objective tests. A resident of a Contracting State that satisfies one of the tests will receive benefits regardless of its motivations in choosing its particular business structure.

The structure of the revised Article is as follows: Paragraph 1 states the general rule that residents are entitled to benefits otherwise accorded to residents only to the extent provided in the Article. Paragraph 2 lists a series of attributes of a resident of a Contracting State, the presence of any one of which will entitle that person to all the benefits of the Convention. Paragraph 3 provides a derivative benefits rule. Paragraph 4 provides that, regardless of whether a person qualifies for benefits under paragraph 2, benefits may be granted to that person with regard to certain income earned in the conduct of an active trade or business. Paragraph 5 provides a test for headquarters companies. Paragraph 6 provides a special rule for so-called "triangular cases" notwithstanding the other provisions of the Article. Paragraph 7 provides that benefits also may be granted if the competent authority of the State from which benefits are claimed determines that it is appropriate to provide benefits in that case. Paragraph 8 defines certain terms used in the Article.

*Paragraph 1*

Paragraph 1 provides that a resident of a Contracting State will be entitled to the benefits otherwise accorded to residents of a Contracting State under the Convention only to the extent provided in the Article. The benefits otherwise accorded to residents under the Convention include all limitations on source-based taxation under Articles 6 (Income from Real Property) through Article 21 (Other Income), the treaty-based relief from double taxation provided by Article 23 (Relief from Double Taxation), and the protection afforded to residents of a Contracting State under Article 24 (Non-Discrimination). Some provisions do not require that a person be a resident in order to enjoy the benefits of those provisions. For example, Article 25 (Mutual Agreement Procedure) is not limited to residents of the Contracting States, and Article 27 (Members of Diplomatic Missions and Consular Posts) applies to diplomatic agents or consular officials regardless of residence. Article 22 accordingly does not limit the availability of treaty benefits under these provisions.

Article 22 and the anti-abuse provisions of domestic law complement each other, as Article 22 effectively determines whether an entity has a sufficient nexus to the Contracting State to be treated as a resident for treaty purposes, while domestic anti-abuse provisions (*e.g.*, business purpose, substance-over-form, step transaction or conduit principles) determine whether a particular transaction should be recast in accordance with its substance. Thus, domestic law principles of the source Contracting State may be applied to identify the beneficial owner of an item of income, and Article 22 then will be applied to the beneficial owner to determine if that person is entitled to the benefits of the Convention with respect to such income.

*Paragraph 2*

Paragraph 2 has five subparagraphs, each of which describes a category of residents that will be considered qualified persons.

It is intended that the provisions of paragraph 2 will be self-executing. Unlike the provisions of paragraph 7, discussed below, claiming benefits under paragraph 2 does not require advance competent authority ruling or approval. The tax authorities may, of course, on review, determine that the taxpayer has improperly interpreted the paragraph and is not entitled to the benefits claimed.

*Individuals -- Subparagraph 2(a)*

Subparagraph 2(a) provides that individual residents of a Contracting State will be considered qualified persons. If such an individual receives income as a nominee on behalf of a third country resident, benefits may be denied under the respective articles of the Convention by the requirement that the beneficial owner of the income be a resident of a Contracting State.

*Governments -- Subparagraph 2(b)*

Subparagraph 2(b) provides that the Contracting States and any political subdivision or local authority or instrumentality thereof will be considered qualified persons.

*Publicly-Traded Corporations -- Subparagraph 2(c)(i)*

Subparagraph 2(c) applies to two categories of companies: publicly traded companies and subsidiaries of publicly traded companies. A company resident in a Contracting State will be considered a qualified person under clause (i) of subparagraph (c) if the principal class of its shares, and any disproportionate class of shares, is regularly traded on one or more recognized stock exchanges and the company satisfies at least one of the following additional requirements. First, under clause (A) in the case of a company resident in Poland, the company's principal class of shares must be primarily traded on one or more recognized stock exchanges located either in Poland or within the European Union, and in the case of a company resident in the United States, the company's principal class or shares must be primarily traded on a recognized stock exchange located either in the United States or in another state that is a party to the North American Free Trade Agreement. If the company's principal class of shares does not satisfy the trading requirement set forth in clause (A), clause (B) provides that the regularly-traded company can nevertheless satisfy the requirements of clause (i) if the company's primary place of management and control is in its State of residence.

The term "recognized stock exchange" is defined in subparagraph 8(a). It includes (i) any stock exchange registered with the Securities and Exchange Commission as a national securities exchange for purposes of the Securities Exchange Act of 1934; (ii) the Warsaw Stock Exchange; (iii) the stock exchanges of Amsterdam, Brussels, Budapest, Frankfurt, London, Mexico City, Montreal, Paris, Toronto, Vienna and Zurich, and (iv) any other stock exchange agreed upon by the competent authorities of the Contracting States.

If a company has only one class of shares, it is only necessary to consider whether the shares of that class meet the relevant trading requirements. If the company has more than one class of shares, it is necessary as an initial matter to determine which class or classes constitute the "principal class of shares". The term "principal class of shares" is defined in subparagraph 8(b) to mean the ordinary or common shares of the company representing the majority of the aggregate voting power and value of the company. If the company does not have a class of ordinary or common shares representing the majority of the aggregate voting power and value of the company, then the "principal class of shares" is that class or any combination of classes of shares that represents, in the aggregate, a majority of the voting power and value of the company. Although in a particular case involving a company with several classes of shares it is conceivable that more than one group of classes could be identified that account for more than 50% of the shares, it is only necessary for one such group to satisfy the requirements of this subparagraph in order for the company to be entitled to benefits. Benefits would not be denied to the company even if a second, non-qualifying, group of shares with more than half of the company's voting power and value could be identified.

A company whose principal class of shares is regularly traded on a recognized stock exchange will nevertheless not be considered a qualified person under subparagraph 2(c) if it has a disproportionate class of shares that is not regularly traded on a recognized stock exchange. The term "disproportionate class of shares" is defined in subparagraph 8(c). A company has a disproportionate class of shares if it has outstanding a class of shares which is subject to terms or other arrangements that entitle the holder to a larger portion of the company's income, profit, or gain in the other Contracting State than that to which the holder would be entitled in the absence of such terms or arrangements. Thus, for example, a company resident in Poland has a disproportionate class of shares if it has outstanding a class of "tracking stock" that pays dividends based upon a formula that approximates the company's return on its assets employed in the United States.

The following example illustrates this result.

Example. OCo is a corporation resident in Poland. OCo has two classes of shares: Common and Preferred. The Common shares are listed and regularly traded on the Warsaw Stock Exchange. The Preferred shares have no voting rights and are entitled to receive dividends equal in amount to interest payments that OCo receives from unrelated borrowers in the United States. The Preferred shares are owned entirely by a single investor that is a resident of a country with which the United States does not have a tax treaty. The Common shares account for more than 50 percent of the value of OCo and for 100 percent of the voting power. Because the owner of the Preferred shares is entitled to receive payments corresponding to the U.S. source interest income earned by OCo, the Preferred shares are a disproportionate class of shares. Because the Preferred shares are not regularly traded on a recognized stock exchange, OCo will not qualify for benefits under subparagraph (c) of paragraph 2.

The term "regularly traded" is not defined in the Convention. In accordance with paragraph 2 of Article 3 (General Definitions), this term will be defined by reference to the domestic tax laws of the State from which treaty benefits are sought, generally the source State. In the case of the United States, this term is understood to have the meaning it has under Treas. Reg. section 1.884-5(d)(4)(i)(B), relating to the branch tax provisions of the Code. Under these regulations, a class of shares is considered to be "regularly traded" if two requirements are met: trades in the class of shares are made in more than *de minimis* quantities on at least 60 days during the taxable year, and the aggregate number of shares in the class traded during the year is at least 10 percent of the average number of shares outstanding during the year. Sections 1.884-5(d)(4)(i)(A), (ii) and (iii) will not be taken into account for purposes of defining the term "regularly traded" under the Convention.

The regular trading requirement can be met by trading on any recognized exchange or exchanges located in either State. Trading on one or more recognized stock exchanges may be aggregated for purposes of this requirement. Thus, a U.S. company could satisfy the regularly traded requirement through trading, in whole or in part, on any recognized stock exchange. Authorized but unissued shares are not considered for purposes of this test.

The term "primarily traded" is defined in subparagraph 8(d). The shares of a company shall be considered "primarily traded" on a recognized stock exchange if the number of shares in the company's principal class of shares that are traded during the taxable year on all recognized stock exchanges in the Contracting State of which the company is a resident (or in the case of a company resident in Poland, on a recognized stock exchange located within the European Union or in any other European Free Trade Association (EFTA) state, or in the case of a company resident in the United States, on a recognized stock exchange located in another state that is a party to the North American Free Trade Agreement (NAFTA)) exceeds the number of shares in the company's principal class of shares that are traded during that year on established securities markets in any other single foreign country. This treaty-based definition is consistent with meaning of the term under Treas. Reg. section 1.884-5(d)(3), relating to the branch tax provisions of the Code.

A company whose principal class of shares is regularly traded on a recognized exchange but cannot meet the primarily traded test may claim treaty benefits if its primary place of management and control is in its country of residence. This test is distinct from the "place of effective management" test which is used in the OECD Model and by many other countries to establish residence. In some cases, the place of effective management test has been interpreted to mean the place where the board of directors meets. By contrast, the primary place of management and control test looks to where day-to-day responsibility for the management of the company (and its subsidiaries) is exercised. The company's primary place of management and control will be located in the State in which the company is a resident only if the executive officers and senior management employees exercise day-to-day responsibility for more of the strategic, financial and operational policy decision making for the company (including direct and indirect subsidiaries) in that State than in the other State or any third state, and the staff that support the management in making those decisions are also based in that State. Thus, the test looks to the overall activities of the relevant persons to see where those activities are conducted. In most cases, it will be a necessary, but not a sufficient, condition that the headquarters of the company (that is, the place at which the CEO and other top executives normally are based) be located in the Contracting State of which the company is a resident.

To apply the test, it will be necessary to determine which persons are to be considered "executive officers and senior management employees". In most cases, it will not be necessary to look beyond the executives who are members of the Board of Directors (the "inside directors") in the case of a U.S. company. That will not always be the case, however; in fact, the relevant persons may be employees of subsidiaries if those persons make the strategic, financial and operational policy decisions. Moreover, it would be necessary to take into account any special voting arrangements that result in certain board members making certain decisions without the participation of other board members.

*Subsidiaries of Publicly-Traded Corporations -- Subparagraph 2(c)(ii)*

A company resident in a Contracting State is entitled to all the benefits of the Convention under clause (ii) of subparagraph (c) of paragraph 2 if five or fewer publicly traded companies described in clause (i) are the direct or indirect owners of at least 50 percent of the aggregate vote and value of the company's shares (and at least 50 percent of any disproportionate class of shares). If the publicly-traded companies are indirect owners, however, each of the intermediate companies must be a resident of one of the Contracting States.

Thus, for example, a company that is a resident of Poland, all the shares of which are owned by another company that is a resident of Poland, would qualify for benefits under the Convention if the principal class of shares (and any disproportionate classes of shares) of the parent company are regularly and primarily traded on a recognized stock exchange in Poland (or within the European Union or EFTA). However, such a subsidiary would not qualify for benefits under clause (ii) if the publicly traded parent company were a resident of a third state,

66

for example, and not a resident of the United States or Poland. Furthermore, if a parent company in Poland indirectly owned the bottom-tier company through a chain of subsidiaries, each such subsidiary in the chain, as an intermediate owner, must be a resident of the United States or Poland in order for the subsidiary to meet the test in clause (ii).

*Tax Exempt Organizations -- Subparagraph 2(d)*

Subparagraph 2(d) provides rules by which the tax exempt organizations described in paragraph 2 of Article 4 (Resident) will be considered qualified persons. A pension fund will qualify for benefits if more than fifty percent of the beneficiaries, members or participants of the organization are individuals resident in either Contracting State. For purposes of this provision, the term "beneficiaries" should be understood to refer to the persons receiving benefits from the organization. On the other hand, a tax-exempt organization other than a pension fund automatically qualifies for benefits, without regard to the residence of its beneficiaries or members. Entities qualifying under this rule generally are those that are exempt from tax in their State of residence and that are organized and operated exclusively to fulfill religious, charitable, scientific, artistic, cultural, or educational purposes.

*Ownership/Base Erosion -- Subparagraph 2(e)*

Subparagraph 2(e) provides an additional method to qualify for treaty benefits that applies to any form of legal entity that is a resident of a Contracting State. The test provided in subparagraph (e), the so-called ownership and base erosion test, is a two-part test. Both prongs of the test must be satisfied for the resident to be entitled to treaty benefits under subparagraph 2(e).

The ownership prong of the test, under clause (i), requires that 50 percent or more of each class of shares or other beneficial interests in the person is owned, directly or indirectly, on at least half the days of the person's taxable year by persons who are residents of the Contracting State of which that person is a resident and that are themselves entitled to treaty benefits under subparagraphs (a), (b), (d) or clause (i) of subparagraph (c) of paragraph 2. In the case of indirect owners, however, each of the intermediate owners must be a resident of that Contracting State.

Trusts may be entitled to benefits under this provision if they are treated as residents under Article 4 (Residence) and they otherwise satisfy the requirements of this subparagraph. For purposes of this subparagraph, the beneficial interests in a trust will be considered to be owned by its beneficiaries in proportion to each beneficiary's actuarial interest in the trust. The interest of a remainder beneficiary will be equal to 100 percent less the aggregate percentages held by income beneficiaries. A beneficiary's interest in a trust will not be considered to be owned by a person entitled to benefits under the other provisions of paragraph 2 if it is not possible to determine the beneficiary's actuarial interest. Consequently, if it is not possible to determine the actuarial interest of the beneficiaries in a trust, the ownership test under clause (i) cannot be satisfied, unless all possible beneficiaries are persons entitled to benefits under the other subparagraphs of paragraph 2.

67

The base erosion prong of clause (ii) of subparagraph (e) is satisfied with respect to a person if less than 50 percent of the person's gross income for the taxable year, as determined under the tax law in the person's State of residence, is paid or accrued to persons who are not residents of either Contracting State entitled to benefits under subparagraphs (a), (b), (d) or clause (i) of subparagraph (c) of paragraph 2, in the form of payments deductible for tax purposes in the payer's State of residence. These amounts do not include arm's-length payments in the ordinary course of business for services or tangible property. To the extent they are deductible from the taxable base, trust distributions are deductible payments. However, depreciation and amortization deductions, which do not represent payments or accruals to other persons, are disregarded for this purpose.

*Paragraph 3*

Paragraph 3 sets forth a "derivative benefits" test that is potentially applicable to all treaty benefits, although the test is applied to individual items of income. In general, a derivative benefits test entitles certain companies that are residents of a Contracting State to treaty benefits if the owner of the company would have been entitled to the same benefit had the income in question flowed directly to that owner. To qualify under this paragraph, the company must meet an ownership test and a base erosion test.

Subparagraph 3(a) sets forth the ownership test. Under this test, seven or fewer equivalent beneficiaries must own shares representing at least 95 percent of the aggregate voting power and value of the company and at least 50 percent of any disproportionate class of shares. Ownership may be direct or indirect.

The term "equivalent beneficiary" is defined in subparagraph 8(f). This definition may be met in two alternative ways.

Under the first alternative, a person may be an equivalent beneficiary because it is entitled to equivalent benefits under a tax treaty between the country of source and the country in which the person is a resident. This alternative has two requirements.

The first requirement as set forth in clause (i) of subparagraph 8(f) is that the person must be a resident of a member state of the European Union or any other European Free Trade Association (EFTA) state or of a party to the North American Free Trade Agreement (collectively, "qualifying States"). In addition, the person must be entitled to all the benefits of a comprehensive tax treaty between the Contracting State from which benefits of the Convention are claimed and a qualifying state under provisions that are analogous to the rules in subparagraphs 2(a), 2(b), 2(c)(i), or 2(d) of this Article. If the treaty in question does not have a comprehensive limitation on benefits article, this requirement is met only if the person would be entitled to treaty benefits under the tests in subparagraphs 2(a), 2(b), 2(c)(i), or 2(d) of this Article if the person were a resident of one of the Contracting States.

Clause (i)(B) of subparagraph 8(f) requires that with respect to, dividends, interest, and royalties, the person must be entitled to a rate of tax that is at least as low as the tax rate that would apply under the Convention to such income. Thus, the rates to be compared are: (1) the rate of tax that the source State would have imposed if a qualified resident of the other

Contracting State was the beneficial owner of the income; and (2) the rate of tax that the source State would have imposed if the third state resident had received the income directly from the source State.

Subparagraph 8(g) provides a special rule to take account of the fact that withholding taxes on many inter-company dividends, interest and royalties are exempt within the European Union by reason of various EU directives, rather than by tax treaty. If a U.S. company receives such payments from a Polish company, and that U.S. company is owned by a company resident in a member state of the European Union that would have qualified for an exemption from withholding tax if it had received the income directly, the parent company will be treated as an equivalent beneficiary. This rule is necessary because many European Union member countries have not re-negotiated their tax treaties to reflect the exemptions available under the directives.

The requirement that a person be entitled to "all the benefits" of a comprehensive tax treaty eliminates those persons that qualify for benefits with respect to only certain types of income. Accordingly, the fact that a French parent of a Polish company is engaged in the active conduct of a trade or business in France and therefore would be entitled to the benefits of the U.S.-France treaty if it received dividends directly from a U.S. subsidiary of the Polish company will not qualify such French company as an equivalent beneficiary. Further, the French company cannot be an equivalent beneficiary if it qualifies for benefits only with respect to certain income as a result of a "derivative benefits" provision in the U.S.-France treaty. However, because such French company is a resident of a qualifying state, it would be possible to look through the French company to its parent company to determine whether the parent company is an equivalent beneficiary.

The second alternative for satisfying the "equivalent beneficiary" test is available only to residents of one of the two Contracting States. U.S. or Polish residents who are eligible for treaty benefits by reason of subparagraphs 2(a), 2(b), 2(c)(i), or 2(d) are equivalent beneficiaries for purposes of the relevant tests in this Article. Thus, a Polish individual will be an equivalent beneficiary without regard to whether the individual would have been entitled to receive the same benefits if it received the income directly. A resident of a third country cannot qualify for treaty benefits under these provisions by reason of those paragraphs or any other rule of the treaty, and therefore does not qualify as an equivalent beneficiary under this alternative. Thus, a resident of a third country can be an equivalent beneficiary only if it would have been entitled to equivalent benefits had it received the income directly.

The second alternative was included in order to clarify that ownership by certain residents of a Contracting State would not disqualify a U.S. or Polish company under this paragraph. Thus, for example, if 90 percent of a Polish company is owned by five companies that are resident in member states of the European Union who satisfy the requirements of subparagraph 8(g)(i), and 10 percent of the Polish company is owned by a U.S. or Polish individual, then the Polish company still can satisfy the requirements of subparagraph 3(a).

Subparagraph 3(b) sets forth the base erosion test. A company meets this base erosion test if less than 50 percent of its gross income (as determined in the company's State of residence) for the taxable period is paid or accrued, directly or indirectly, to a person or persons who are not equivalent beneficiaries in the form of payments deductible for tax purposes in company's State of residence. These amounts do not include arm's-length payments in the ordinary course of business for services or tangible property. This test is qualitatively the same as the base erosion test in subparagraph 2(e)(ii), except that the test in paragraph 3(b) focuses on base-eroding payments to persons who are not equivalent beneficiaries.

*Paragraph 4*

Paragraph 4 sets forth an alternative test under which a resident of a Contracting State may receive treaty benefits with respect to certain items of income that are connected to an active trade or business conducted in its State of residence. A resident of a Contracting State may qualify for benefits under paragraph 4 whether or not it also qualifies under paragraph 2 or 3.

Subparagraph 4(a) sets forth the general rule that a resident of a Contracting State engaged in the active conduct of a trade or business in that State may obtain the benefits of the Convention with respect to an item of income derived in the other Contracting State. The item of income, however, must be derived in connection with or incidental to that trade or business.

The term "trade or business" is not defined in the Convention. Pursuant to paragraph 2 of Article 3 (General Definitions), when determining whether a resident of Poland is entitled to the benefits of the Convention under paragraph 3 of this Article with respect to an item of income derived from sources within the United States, the United States will ascribe to this term the meaning that it has under the law of the United States. Accordingly, the U.S. competent authority will refer to the regulations issued under Code section 367(a) for the definition of the term "trade or business." In general, therefore, a trade or business will be considered to be a specific unified group of activities that constitutes or could constitute an independent economic enterprise carried on for profit. Furthermore, a corporation generally will be considered to carry on a trade or business only if the officers and employees of the corporation conduct substantial managerial and operational activities.

The business of making or managing investments for the resident's own account will be considered to be a trade or business only when part of banking, insurance or securities activities conducted by a bank, an insurance company, or a registered securities dealer respectively. Such activities conducted by a person other than a bank, insurance company or registered securities dealer will not be considered to be the conduct of an active trade or business, nor would they be considered to be the conduct of an active trade or business if conducted by a bank, insurance company or registered securities dealer but not as part of the company's banking, insurance or dealer business. Because a headquarters operation is in the business of managing investments, a company that functions solely as a headquarters company will not be considered to be engaged in an active trade or business for purposes of paragraph 4.

An item of income is derived in connection with a trade or business if the income-producing activity in the State of source is a line of business that "forms a part of" or is "complementary" to the trade or business conducted in the State of residence by the income recipient.

A business activity generally will be considered to form part of a business activity conducted in the State of source if the two activities involve the design, manufacture or sale of the same products or type of products, or the provision of similar services. The line of business in the State of residence may be upstream, downstream, or parallel to the activity conducted in the State of source. Thus, the line of business may provide inputs for a manufacturing process that occurs in the State of source, may sell the output of that manufacturing process, or simply may sell the same sorts of products that are being sold by the trade or business carried on in the State of source.

Example 1. USCo is a corporation resident in the United States. USCo is engaged in an active manufacturing business in the United States. USCo owns 100 percent of the shares of FCo, a corporation resident in Poland. FCo distributes USCo products in Poland. Since the business activities conducted by the two corporations involve the same products, FCo's distribution business is considered to form a part of USCo's manufacturing business.

Example 2. The facts are the same as in Example 1, except that USCo does not manufacture. Rather, USCo operates a large research and development facility in the United States that licenses intellectual property to affiliates worldwide, including FCo. FCo and other USCo affiliates then manufacture and market the USCo-designed products in their respective markets. Since the activities conducted by FCo and USCo involve the same product lines, these activities are considered to form a part of the same trade or business.

For two activities to be considered to be "complementary," the activities need not relate to the same types of products or services, but they should be part of the same overall industry and be related in the sense that the success or failure of one activity will tend to result in success or failure for the other. Where more than one trade or business is conducted in the State of source and only one of the trades or businesses forms a part of or is complementary to a trade or business conducted in the State of residence, it is necessary to identify the trade or business to which an item of income is attributable. Royalties generally will be considered to be derived in connection with the trade or business to which the underlying intangible property is attributable. Dividends will be deemed to be derived first out of earnings and profits of the treaty-benefited trade or business, and then out of other earnings and profits. Interest income may be allocated under any reasonable method consistently applied. A method that conforms to U.S. principles for expense allocation will be considered a reasonable method.

Example 3. Americair is a corporation resident in the United States that operates an international airline. FSub is a wholly-owned subsidiary of Americair resident in Poland. FSub operates a chain of hotels in Poland that are located near airports served by Americair flights. Americair frequently sells tour packages that include air travel to Polnd and lodging at FSub hotels. Although both companies are engaged in the active conduct of a trade or business, the businesses of operating a chain of hotels and operating an airline are distinct trades or businesses. Therefore FSub's business does not form a part of Americair's business. However, FSub's business is considered to be complementary to Americair's business because they are part of the same overall industry (travel) and the links between their operations tend to make them interdependent.

Example 4. The facts are the same as in Example 3, except that FSub owns an office building in Poland instead of a hotel chain. No part of Americair's business is conducted through the office building. FSub's business is not considered to form a part of or to be complementary to Americair's business. They are engaged in distinct trades or businesses in separate industries, and there is no economic dependence between the two operations.

Example 5. USFlower is a corporation resident in the United States. USFlower produces and sells flowers in the United States and other countries. USFlower owns all the shares of ForHolding, a corporation resident in Poland. ForHolding is a holding company that is not engaged in a trade or business. ForHolding owns all the shares of three corporations that are resident in Poland: ForFlower, ForLawn, and ForFish. ForFlower distributes USFlower flowers under the USFlower trademark in Poland. ForLawn markets a line of lawn care products in Poland under the USFlower trademark. In addition to being sold under the same trademark, ForLawn and ForFlower products are sold in the same stores and sales of each company's products tend to generate increased sales of the other's products. ForFish imports fish from the United States and distributes it to fish wholesalers in Poland. For purposes of paragraph 3, the business of ForFlower forms a part of the business of USFlower, the business of ForLawn is complementary to the business of USFlower, and the business of ForFish is neither part of nor complementary to that of USFlower.

An item of income derived from the State of source is "incidental to" the trade or business carried on in the State of residence if production of the item facilitates the conduct of the trade or business in the State of residence. An example of incidental income is the temporary investment of working capital of a person in the State of residence in securities issued by persons in the State of source.

Subparagraph (b) of paragraph 4 states a further condition to the general rule in subparagraph (a) in cases where the trade or business generating the item of income in question is carried on either by the person deriving the income or by any associated enterprises. Subparagraph (b) states that the trade or business carried on in the State of residence, under these circumstances, must be substantial in relation to the activity in the State of source. The substantiality requirement is intended to prevent a narrow case of treaty-shopping abuses in which a company attempts to qualify for benefits by engaging in de minimis connected business activities in the treaty country in which it is resident (i.e., activities that have little economic cost or effect with respect to the company business as a whole).

The determination of substantiality is made based upon all the facts and circumstances and takes into account the comparative sizes of the trades or businesses in each Contracting State, the nature of the activities performed in each Contracting State and the relative contributions made to that trade or business in each Contracting State. In any case, in making each determination or comparison, due regard will be given to the relative sizes of the economies in the two Contracting States.

The determination in subparagraph (b) also is made separately for each item of income derived from the State of source. It therefore is possible that a person would be entitled to the benefits of the Convention with respect to one item of income but not with respect to another. If a resident of a Contracting State is entitled to treaty benefits with respect to a particular item of income under paragraph 4, the resident is entitled to all benefits of the Convention insofar as they affect the taxation of that item of income in the State of source.

The application of the substantiality requirement only to income from related parties focuses only on potential abuse cases, and does not hamper certain other kinds of non-abusive activities, even though the income recipient resident in a Contracting State may be very small in relation to the entity generating income in the other Contracting State. For example, if a small U.S. research firm develops a process that it licenses to a very large, unrelated, pharmaceutical manufacturer in Poland, the size of the U.S. research firm would not have to be tested against the size of the manufacturer. Similarly, a small U.S. bank that makes a loan to a very large unrelated company operating a business in Poland would not have to pass a substantiality test to receive treaty benefits under paragraph 4.

Subparagraph (c) of paragraph 3 provides special attribution rules for purposes of applying the substantive rules of subparagraphs (a) and (b). Thus, these rules apply for purposes of determining whether a person meets the requirement in subparagraph (a) that it be engaged in the active conduct of a trade or business and that the item of income is derived in connection with that active trade or business, and for making the comparison required by the "substantiality" requirement in subparagraph (b). Subparagraph (c) attributes to a person activities conducted by persons "connected" to such person. A person ("X") is connected to another person ("Y") if X possesses 50 percent or more of the beneficial interest in Y (or if Y possesses 50 percent or more of the beneficial interest in X). For this purpose, X is connected to a company if X owns shares representing fifty percent or more of the aggregate voting power and value of the company or fifty percent or more of the beneficial equity interest in the company. X also is connected to Y if a third person possesses fifty percent or more of the beneficial interest in both X and Y. For this purpose, if X or Y is a company, the threshold relationship with respect to such company or companies is fifty percent or more of the aggregate voting power and value or fifty percent or more of the beneficial equity interest. Finally, X is connected to Y if, based upon all the facts and circumstances, X controls Y, Y controls X, or X and Y are controlled by the same person or persons.

*Paragraph 5*

Paragraph 5 provides that a resident of one of the Contracting States is entitled to all the benefits of the Convention if that person functions as a recognized headquarters company for a multinational corporate group. The provisions of this paragraph are consistent with the other U.S. tax treaties where this provision has been adopted. For this purpose, the multinational corporate group includes all corporations that the headquarters company supervises, and excludes affiliated corporations not supervised by the headquarters company. The headquarters company does not have to own shares in the companies that it supervises. In order to be considered a headquarters company, the person must meet several requirements that are enumerated in paragraph 5. These requirements are discussed below.

*Overall Supervision and Administration*

Subparagraph 5(a) provides that the person must provide a substantial portion of the overall supervision and administration of the group. This activity may include group financing, but group financing may not be the principal activity of the person functioning as the headquarters company. A person only will be considered to engage in supervision and administration if it engages in a number of the following activities: group financing, pricing, marketing, internal auditing, internal communications, and management. Other activities also could be part of the function of supervision and administration.

In determining whether a "substantial portion" of the overall supervision and administration of the group is provided by the headquarters company, its headquarters-related activities must be substantial in relation to the same activities for the same group performed by other entities. Subparagraph 5(a) does not require that the group that is supervised include persons in the other State. However, it is anticipated that in most cases the group will include such persons, due to the requirement in subparagraph 5(g), discussed below, that the income derived in the other Contracting State by the headquarters company be derived in connection with or be incidental to an active trade or business supervised by the headquarters company.

*Active Trade or Business*

Subparagraph 5(b) is the first of several requirements intended to ensure that the relevant group is truly "multinational." This subparagraph provides that the corporate group supervised by the headquarters company must consist of corporations resident in, and engaged in active trades or businesses in, at least five countries. Furthermore, at least five countries must each contribute substantially to the income generated by the group, as the rule requires that the business activities carried on in each of the five countries (or groupings of countries) generate at least 10 percent of the gross income of the group. For purposes of the 10 percent gross income requirement, the income from multiple countries may be aggregated into non-overlapping groupings, as long as there are at least five individual countries or groupings that each satisfies the 10 percent requirement. If the gross income requirement under this subparagraph is not met for a taxable year, the taxpayer may satisfy this requirement by applying the 10 percent gross income test to the average of the gross incomes for the four years preceding the taxable year.

*Example.* PHQ is a corporation resident in Poland. PHQ functions as a headquarters company for a group of companies. These companies are resident in the United States, Canada, New Zealand, the United Kingdom, Malaysia, the Philippines, Singapore, and Indonesia. The gross income generated by each of these companies for 2012 and 2013 is as follows:

| Country | 2012 | 2013 |
|---|---|---|
| United States | $40 | $45 |
| Canada | $25 | $15 |
| New Zealand | $10 | $20 |
| United Kingdom | $30 | $35 |
| Malaysia | $10 | $12 |

| | | |
|---|---|---|
| Philippines | $7 | $10 |
| Singapore | $10 | $8 |
| Indonesia | $5 | $10 |
| Total | $137 | $155 |

For 2012, 10 percent of the gross income of this group is equal to $13.70. Only the United States, Canada, and the United Kingdom satisfy this requirement for that year. The other countries may be aggregated to meet this requirement. Because New Zealand and Malaysia have a total gross income of $20, and the Philippines, Singapore, and Indonesia have a total gross income of $22, these two groupings of countries may be treated as the fourth and fifth members of the group for purposes of subparagraph 5(b).

In the following year, 10 percent of the gross income is $15.50. Only the United States, New Zealand, and the United Kingdom satisfy this requirement. Because Canada and Malaysia have a total gross income of $27, and the Philippines, Singapore, and Indonesia have a total gross income of $28, these two groupings of countries may be treated as the fourth and fifth members of the group for purposes of subparagraph 5(b). The fact that Canada replaced New Zealand in a group is not relevant for this purpose. The composition of the grouping may change from year to year.

*Single Country Limitation*

Subparagraph 5(c) provides that the business activities carried on in any one country other than the headquarters company's State of residence must generate less than 50 percent of the gross income of the group. If the gross income requirement under this subparagraph is not met for a taxable year, the taxpayer may satisfy this requirement by applying the 50 percent gross income test to the average of the gross incomes for the four years preceding the taxable year. The following example illustrates the application of this clause.

*Example.* PHQ is a corporation resident in Poland. PHQ functions as a headquarters company for a group of companies. PHQ derives dividend income from a United States subsidiary in the 2008 taxable year. The state of residence of each of these companies, the situs of their activities and the amounts of gross income attributable to each for the years 2008 through 2012 are set forth below.

| Country | Situs | 2012 | 2011 | 2010 | 2009 | 2008 |
|---|---|---|---|---|---|---|
| United States | U.S. | $100 | $100 | $95 | $90 | $85 |
| Mexico | U.S. | $10 | $8 | $5 | $0 | $0 |
| Canada | U.S. | $20 | $18 | $16 | $15 | $12 |
| United Kingdom | U.K | $30 | $32 | $30 | $28 | $27 |
| New Zealand | N.Z. | $35 | $42 | $38 | $36 | $35 |
| Japan | Japan | $35 | $32 | $30 | $30 | $28 |
| Singapore | Singapore | $30 | $25 | $24 | $22 | $20 |
| Total | | $260 | $257 | $238 | $221 | $207 |

Because the United States' total gross income of $130 in 2012 is not less than 50 percent of the gross income of the group, subparagraph 5(c) is not satisfied with respect to dividends derived in 2012. However, the United States' average gross income for the preceding four years may be used in lieu of the preceding year's average. The United States' average gross income for the years 2008-11 is $111.00 ($444/4). The group's total average gross income for these years is $230.75 ($923/4). Because $111 represents 48.1 percent of the group's average gross income for the years 2008 through 2011, the requirement under subparagraph 5(c) is satisfied.

*Other State Gross Income Limitation*

Subparagraph 5(d) provides that no more than 25 percent of the headquarters company's gross income may be derived from the other Contracting State. Thus, if the headquarters company's gross income for the taxable year is $200, no more than $50 of this amount may be derived from the other Contracting State. If the gross income requirement under this subparagraph is not met for a taxable year, the taxpayer may satisfy this requirement by applying the 25 percent gross income test to the average of the gross incomes for the four years preceding the taxable year.

*Independent Discretionary Authority*

Subparagraph 5(e) requires that the headquarters company have and exercise independent discretionary authority to carry out the functions referred to in subparagraph 5(a). Thus, if the headquarters company was nominally responsible for group financing, pricing, marketing and other management functions, but merely implemented instructions received from another entity, the headquarters company would not be considered to have and exercise independent discretionary authority with respect to these functions. This determination is made individually for each function. For instance, a headquarters company could be nominally responsible for group financing, pricing, marketing and internal auditing functions, but another entity could be actually directing the headquarters company as to the group financing function. In such a case, the headquarters company would not be deemed to have independent discretionary authority for group financing, but it might have such authority for the other functions. Functions for which the headquarters company does not have and exercise independent discretionary authority are considered to be conducted by an entity other than the headquarters company for purposes of subparagraph 5(a).

*Income Taxation Rules*

Subparagraph 2(f) requires that the headquarters company be subject to the generally applicable income taxation rules in its country of residence. This reference should be understood to mean that the company must be subject to the income taxation rules to which a company engaged in the active conduct of a trade or business would be subject. Thus, if one of the Contracting States has or introduces special taxation legislation that imposes a lower rate of income tax on headquarters companies than is imposed on companies engaged in the active conduct of a trade or business, or provides for an artificially low taxable base for such companies, a headquarters company subject to these rules is not entitled to the benefits of the Convention under paragraph 5.

*In Connection With or Incidental to Trade or Business*

Subparagraph 5(g) requires that the income derived in the other Contracting State be derived in connection with or be incidental to the active business activities referred to subparagraph 5(b). This determination is made under the principles set forth in paragraph 3. For instance, assume that a Polish company satisfies the other requirements in paragraph 5 and acts as a headquarters company for a group that includes a U.S. corporation. If the group is engaged in the design and manufacture of computer software, but the U.S. corporation is also engaged in the design and manufacture of photocopying machines, the income that the Polish company derives from the United States would have to be derived in connection with or be incidental to the income generated by the computer business in order to be entitled to the benefits of the Convention under paragraph 5. Interest income received from the U.S. corporation also would be entitled to the benefits of the Convention under this subparagraph as long as the interest was attributable to the computer business supervised by the headquarters company. Interest income derived from an unrelated party would normally not, however, satisfy the requirements of this clause.

*Paragraph 6*

Paragraph 6 deals with the treatment of income in the context of a so-called "triangular case." The term "triangular case" refers to the use of a structure like the one described in the following paragraph by a resident of Poland to earn income from the United States:

A resident of Poland, who would, absent paragraph 6, qualify for benefits under one or more of the provisions of this Article, sets up a permanent establishment in a third state that imposes a low or zero rate of tax on the income of the permanent establishment. The resident of Poland lends funds into the United States through the permanent establishment. The permanent establishment, despite its third-jurisdiction location, is an integral part of the resident of Poland. Therefore, the income that it earns on those loans, absent the provisions of paragraph 6, is entitled to exemption from U.S. withholding tax under the Convention. Under a current income tax treaty between Poland and the host jurisdiction of the permanent establishment, the income of the permanent establishment is exempt from tax by Poland (alternatively, Poland may choose to exempt the income of the permanent establishment from income tax). Thus, the interest income, absent paragraph 6, would be exempt from U.S. tax, subject to little or no tax in the host jurisdiction of the permanent establishment, and exempt from tax in Poland.

Paragraph 6 provides that the tax benefits that would otherwise apply under the Convention will not apply to any item of income if the combined aggregate effective tax rate in the residence State and the third state is less than 60 percent of the general rate of company tax applicable in the residence State. In the case of dividends, interest and royalties to which this paragraph applies, the withholding tax rates under the Convention are replaced with a 15 percent withholding tax. Any other income to which the provisions of paragraph 6 apply is subject to tax under the domestic law of the source State, notwithstanding any other provisions of the Convention.

In general, the principles employed under Code section 954(b)(4) will be employed to determine whether the profits are subject to an effective rate of taxation that is above the specified threshold.

Notwithstanding the level of tax on interest and royalty income of the permanent establishment, paragraph 6 will not apply under certain circumstances. In the case of royalties, paragraph 6 will not apply if the royalties are received as compensation for the use of, or the right to use, intangible property produced or developed by the permanent establishment itself. In the case of any other income, paragraph 6 will not apply if that income is derived in connection with, or is incidental to, the active conduct of a trade or business carried on by the permanent establishment in the third state. The business of making, managing or simply holding investments is not considered to be an active trade or business, unless these are securities activities carried on by a registered securities dealer.

Paragraph 6 applies reciprocally. However, the United States does not exempt the profits of a third-jurisdiction permanent establishment of a U.S. resident from U.S. tax, either by statute or by treaty.

*Paragraph 7*

Paragraph 7 provides that a resident of one of the States that is not entitled to the benefits of the Convention as a result of paragraphs 1 through 3 still may be granted benefits under the Convention at the discretion of the competent authority of the State from which benefits are claimed if the resident demonstrates that neither its establishment, acquisition, or maintenance, nor the conduct of its operations, has or had as one of its principal purposes the obtaining of benefits under the Convention. Thus, persons that establish operations in one of the Contracting States with a principal purpose of obtaining the benefits of the Convention will not be granted benefits of the Convention under paragraph 7. In order to be granted benefits under paragraph 7, a company must establish to the satisfaction of the competent authority of the State from which benefits are being claimed clear non-tax business reasons for its formation, acquisition, or maintenance in the other Contracting State, which demonstrate a sufficient nexus or relationship to the other Contracting State, taking into account considerations other than those addressed through the objective tests in paragraphs 1 through 3, and that the allowance of benefits would not otherwise be contrary to the purposes of the Convention. For example, in the case of a resident subsidiary company with a parent in a third state, the fact that the relevant withholding rate provided in the Convention is at least as low as the corresponding withholding rate in the tax treaty between the State of source and the third state is not by itself evidence of a nexus or relationship to the other Contracting State. Similarly, where a foreign corporation is engaged in a portable business such as financing, or where the domestic law of a Contracting State provides a special tax treatment for certain activities conducted offshore (*e.g.,* licensing intangibles) or in special zones, those factors will not be evidence of a non-tax business reason for locating in that State. In such cases, additional favorable business factors must be present to establish a nexus to that State.

The competent authority's discretion is quite broad. It may grant all of the benefits of the Convention to the taxpayer making the request, or it may grant only certain benefits. For instance, it may grant benefits only with respect to a particular item of income in a manner similar to paragraph 3. Further, the competent authority may establish conditions, such as setting time limits on the duration of any relief granted.

For purposes of implementing paragraph 7, a taxpayer will be permitted to present his case to the relevant competent authority for an advance determination based on the facts. In these circumstances, it is also expected that, if the competent authority determines that benefits are to be allowed, they will be allowed retroactively to the time of entry into force of the relevant treaty provision or the establishment of the structure in question, whichever is later.

Finally, there may be cases in which a resident of a Contracting State may apply for discretionary relief to the competent authority of his State of residence. This would arise, for example, if the benefit it is claiming is provided by the residence country, and not by the source country. So, for example, if a company that is a resident of the United States would like to claim the benefit of the re-sourcing rule of paragraph 3 of Article 23, but it does not meet any of the objective tests of paragraphs 2 and 3, it may apply to the U.S. competent authority for discretionary relief.

*Paragraph 8*

Paragraph 8 defines several key terms for purposes of the Article. Each of the defined terms is discussed above in the context in which it is used.

## ARTICLE 23 (RELIEF FROM DOUBLE TAXATION)

This Article describes the manner in which each Contracting State undertakes to relieve double taxation. The United States uses the foreign tax credit method under its domestic law and by treaty.

*Paragraph 1*

Paragraph 1 provides that Poland will apply two rules to avoid double taxation. First, under subparagraph 1(a), where a resident of Poland derives income which, in accordance with the provisions of this Convention may be taxed in the United States, Poland shall, subject to the provisions of subparagraph 1(b), exempt such income from tax. Second, under subparagraph 1(b), where a resident of Poland derives income or capital gains which, in accordance with the provisions of Articles 10 (Dividends), 11 (Interest), 13 (Royalties), 14 (Capital Gains) or 21 (Other Income) may be taxed in the United States, Poland shall allow as a deduction from the tax on the income or capital gains of that resident an amount equal to the tax paid to the United States. Such deduction shall not, however, exceed that part of the tax, as computed before the deduction is given, which is attributable to such income or capital gains derived from the United States. Subparagraph 1(c) provides a so-called "exemption with progression" rule. Where in accordance with any provision of this Convention, income derived by a resident of Poland is exempt from tax in Poland, Poland may nevertheless, in calculating the amount of tax on the remaining income of such resident, take into account the exempted income.

*Paragraph 2*

The United States agrees, in paragraph 2, to allow to its citizens and residents a credit against U.S. tax for income taxes paid or accrued to Poland. Paragraph 2 also provides that the other Contracting State's covered taxes are income taxes for U.S. purposes.

Subparagraph 2(b) provides for a deemed-paid credit, consistent with section 902 of the Code, to a U.S. corporation in respect of dividends received from a corporation resident in Poland of which the U.S. corporation owns at least 10 percent of the voting stock. This credit is for the tax paid by the corporation to the other Contracting State on the profits out of which the dividends are considered paid.

The credits allowed under paragraph 2 are in accordance with the provisions and subject to the limitations of U.S. law, as that law may be amended over time, so long as the general principle of the Article, that is, the relief of double taxation, is retained. Thus, although the Convention provides for a foreign tax credit, the terms of the credit are generally determined by the U.S. domestic law in effect for the taxable year for which the credit is allowed. *See, e.g.,* Code sections 901-909 and the regulations thereunder. For example, the credit against U.S. tax generally is limited to the amount of U.S. tax due with respect to net foreign source income within the relevant foreign tax credit limitation category (*see,* Code section 904(a) and (d)), and the dollar amount of the credit is determined in accordance with U.S. currency translation rules (*see, e.g.,* Code section 986). Similarly, U.S. law applies to determine carryover periods for excess credits and other inter-year adjustments.

*Paragraph 3*

Paragraph 3 provides that certain items of gross income that would be otherwise treated as from sources within the United States will be treated as from sources within Poland for purposes of paragraph 2. Paragraph 3 is intended to ensure that a U.S. resident can obtain an appropriate amount of U.S. foreign tax credit for income taxes paid to Poland when the Convention assigns to Poland primary taxing rights over an item of gross income.

Accordingly, if the Convention allows Poland to tax an item of gross income (as defined under U.S. law) derived by a resident of the United States, the United States will treat that item of gross income as gross income from sources within Poland for U.S. foreign tax credit purposes. In the case of a U.S.-owned foreign corporation, however, section 904(h)(10) may apply for purposes of determining the U.S. foreign tax credit with respect to income subject to this re-sourcing rule. Section 904(h)(10) generally applies the foreign tax credit limitation separately to re-sourced income. *See also,* Code sections 865(h) and 904(d)(6). Because paragraph 3 applies to items of gross income, not net income, U.S. expense allocation and apportionment rules (*see, e.g.,* Treas. Reg. 1.861-9 and -9T) continue to apply to income resourced under paragraph 3.

*Paragraph 4*

Paragraph 4 provides special rules for the tax treatment in both States of certain types of income derived from U.S. sources by U.S. citizens who are residents of Poland. Since U.S.

citizens, regardless of residence, are subject to United States tax at ordinary progressive rates on their worldwide income, the U.S. tax on the U.S.-source income of a U.S. citizen resident in Poland may exceed the U.S. tax that may be imposed under the Convention on an item of U.S.-source income derived by a resident of Poland who is not a U.S. citizen. The provisions of paragraph 4 ensure that Poland does not bear the cost of U.S. taxation of its citizens who are residents of Poland.

Subparagraph 4(a) provides, with respect to items of income from sources within the United States, special credit rules for the other Contracting State. These rules apply to items of U.S.-source income that would be either exempt from U.S. tax or subject to reduced rates of U.S. tax under the provisions of the Convention if they had been received by a resident of Poland who is not a U.S. citizen. The tax credit allowed under paragraph 4 with respect to such items need not exceed the U.S. tax that may be imposed under the Convention, other than tax imposed solely by reason of the U.S. citizenship of the taxpayer under the provisions of the saving clause of paragraph 4 of Article 1 (General Scope).

For example, if a U.S. citizen resident in Poland receives portfolio dividends from sources within the United States, the foreign tax credit granted by Poland would be limited to 15 percent of the dividend – the U.S. tax that may be imposed under subparagraph 2(b) of Article 10 (Dividends) – even if the shareholder is subject to U.S. net income tax because of his U.S. citizenship.

Subparagraph 4(b) eliminates the potential for double taxation that can arise because subparagraph 4(a) provides that Poland need not provide full relief for the U.S. tax imposed on its citizens resident in the other Contracting State. The subparagraph provides that the United States will credit the income tax paid or accrued to Poland, after the application of subparagraph 4(a). It further provides that in allowing the credit, the United States will not reduce its tax below the amount that is taken into account in Poland in applying subparagraph 4(a).

Since the income described in paragraph 4(a) generally will be U.S. source income, special rules are required to re-source some of the income to Poland in order for the United States to be able to credit the tax paid to the other Contracting State. This re-sourcing is provided for in subparagraph 4(c), which deems the items of income referred to in subparagraph 4(a) to be from foreign sources to the extent necessary to avoid double taxation under paragraph 4(b).

The following two examples illustrate the application of paragraph 4 in the case of a U.S.-source portfolio dividend received by a U.S. citizen resident in Poland. In both examples, the U.S. rate of tax on residents of the Poland, under subparagraph 2(b) of Article 10 (Dividends) of the Convention, is 15 percent. In both examples, the U.S. income tax rate on the U.S. citizen is 35 percent. In example 1, the rate of income tax imposed in Poland on its resident (the U.S. citizen) is 25 percent (below the U.S. rate), and in example 2, the rate imposed on its resident is 40 percent (above the U.S. rate).

|  | Example 1 | Example 2 |
|---|---|---|
| Subparagraph (a) | | |

81

| | | |
|---|---:|---:|
| U.S. dividend declared | $100.00 | $100.00 |
| Notional U.S. withholding tax (Article 10(2)(b)) | 15.00 | 15.00 |
| Taxable income in Poland | 100.00 | 100.00 |
| Polish tax before credit | 25.00 | 40.00 |
| Less: tax credit for notional U.S. withholding tax | 15.00 | 15.00 |
| Net post-credit tax paid to Poland | 10.00 | 25.00 |

Subparagraphs (b) and (c)

| | | |
|---|---:|---:|
| U.S. pre-tax income | $100.00 | $100.00 |
| U.S. pre-credit citizenship tax | 35.00 | 35.00 |
| Notional U.S. withholding tax | 15.00 | 15.00 |
| U.S. tax eligible to be offset by credit | 20.00 | 20.00 |
| Tax paid to Poland | 10.00 | 25.00 |
| Income re-sourced from U.S. to foreign source (see below) | 28.57 | 57.14 |
| U.S. pre-credit tax on re-sourced income | 10.00 | 20.00 |
| U.S. credit for tax paid to Poland | 10.00 | 20.00 |
| Net post-credit U.S. tax | 10.00 | 0.00 |
| Total U.S. tax | 25.00 | 15.00 |

In both examples, in the application of subparagraph 4(a), Poland credits a 15 percent U.S. tax against its residence tax on the U.S. citizen. In the first example, the net tax paid to Poland after the foreign tax credit is $10.00; in the second example, it is $25.00. In the application of subparagraphs 4(b) and 4(c), from the U.S. tax due before credit of $35.00, the United States subtracts the amount of the U.S. source tax of $15.00, against which no U.S. foreign tax credit is allowed. This subtraction ensures that the United States collects the tax that it is due under the Convention as the State of source.

In both examples, given the 35 percent U.S. tax rate, the maximum amount of U.S. tax against which credit for the tax paid to Poland may be claimed is $20 ($35 U.S. tax minus $15 U.S. withholding tax). Initially, all of the income in both examples was from sources within the United States. For a U.S. foreign tax credit to be allowed for the full amount of the tax paid to Poland, an appropriate amount of the income must be re-sourced to Poland under subparagraph 4(c).

The amount that must be re-sourced depends on the amount of tax for which the U.S. citizen is claiming a U.S. foreign tax credit. In example 1, the tax paid to Poland was $10. For this amount to be creditable against U.S. tax, $28.57 ($10 tax divided by 35 percent U.S. tax rate) must be resourced to Poland. When the tax is credited against the $10 of U.S. tax on this resourced income, there is a net U.S. tax of $10 due after credit ($20 U.S. tax eligible to be offset by credit, minus $10 tax paid to the other Contracting State). Thus, in example 1, there is a total of $25 in U.S. tax ($15 U.S. withholding tax plus $10 residual U.S. tax).

In example 2, the tax paid to Poland was $25, but, because the United States subtracts the U.S. withholding tax of $15 from the total U.S. tax of $35, only $20 of U.S. taxes may be offset by taxes paid to Poland. Accordingly, the amount that must be resourced to Poland is limited to the amount necessary to ensure a U.S. foreign tax credit for $20 of tax paid to Poland, or $57.14 ($20 tax paid to Poland divided by 35 percent U.S. tax rate). When the tax paid to Poland is credited against the U.S. tax on this re-sourced income, there is no residual U.S. tax ($20 U.S. tax minus $25 tax paid to the other Contracting State, subject to the U.S. limit of $20). Thus, in example 2, there is a total of $15 in U.S. tax ($15 U.S. withholding tax plus $0 residual U.S. tax). Because the tax paid to Poland was $25 and the U.S. tax eligible to be offset by credit was $20, there is $5 of excess foreign tax credit available for carryover.

The above examples illustrate the application of paragraph 4 to a single item of gross income. However, taxpayers may encounter situations in which they may have to calculate the foreign tax credit on net income, in which case other methodologies could be applied to achieve the intent of paragraph 4.

*Paragraph 5*

Paragraph 5 coordinates the tax systems of the Contracting States to avoid double taxation that could result from the imposition of exit tax regimes on individuals who relinquish citizenship or long-term residence status. In the case of the United States, paragraph 5 addresses the mark-to-market exit tax regime applicable to "covered expatriates" within the meaning of Code section 877A(g)(1). Paragraph 5 would also address any analogous taxes imposed by Poland. This rule is intended to coordinate taxation by the United States and Poland of taxable gains in the case of a timing mismatch. Such a mismatch may occur, for example, where a U.S. citizen or long-term resident (within the meaning of Code section 877(e)(2)) recognizes, for U.S. tax purposes, taxable gain on a deemed sale of all property on the day before the individual expatriates to Poland.

To avoid double taxation, paragraph 5 provides that where an individual who, upon ceasing to be a resident (as determined under paragraph 1 of Article 4 (Resident)) of one Contracting State, is treated for purposes of taxation by that State as having alienated property and is taxed by that State by reason thereof, the individual may elect to be treated for the purposes of taxation by the other Contracting State as having sold and repurchased the property for its fair market value on the day before the expatriation date. The election in paragraph 5 therefore may be available to any U.S. citizen or long-term resident who expatriates from the United States to Poland. The effect of the election will be to give the individual an adjusted basis in Poland for tax purposes equal to the fair market value of the property as of the date of the deemed alienation in the United States, with the result that only post-emigration gain will be subject to tax in Poland when there is an actual alienation of the property while the individual is a resident of Poland.

Individuals may make the election provided by paragraph 5 only with respect to property that is subject to a Contracting State's deemed disposition rules and only with respect to which gain on a deemed alienation is recognized for that Contracting State's tax purposes in the taxable year of the deemed alienation. In the United States, the following types of property are excluded from the deemed disposition rules in the case of individuals who cease to be citizens or long term residents of the United States: (1) an eligible deferred compensation item as defined under Code section 877A(d)(3), and (2) an interest in a non-grantor trust as defined under Code section 877A(f)(3) (unless the individual elects to take the value of the interest in the trust into account pursuant to procedures prescribed by the IRS pursuant to Code section 877A(f)(4)(B)).

If an individual recognizes in one Contracting State losses and gains from the deemed alienation of multiple properties, then the individual must apply this paragraph consistently with respect to all such properties in both Contracting States. An individual who is deemed to have alienated multiple properties may only make the election under this paragraph if the deemed alienation of all such properties results in a net taxable gain. If the deemed alienation of the multiple properties results in a net loss, then an election under this paragraph may not be made with respect to any such properties.

The other Contracting State is only required to provide a basis adjustment to the extent that tax is actually paid in the first-mentioned Contracting State. Thus, to the extent that the deemed alienation of properties results in a net gain, but no tax is actually paid on such gain due to an exclusion provision or other mechanism provided under the domestic law of the first-mentioned Contracting State, the other Contracting State is not required to provide a basis adjustment. Under the domestic law of the United States, Code section 877A(a)(3) provides an exclusion for certain gain up to $600,000 (as indexed for inflation). Poland also is not required to provide a basis adjustment with respect to tax that is deferred pursuant to Code section 877A(b).

*Relationship to other Articles*

By virtue of subparagraph 5(a) of Article 1 (General Scope), Article 23 is not subject to the saving clause of paragraph 4 of Article 1. Thus, the United States will allow a credit to its citizens and residents in accordance with the Article, even if such credit were to provide a benefit not available under the Code (such as the re-sourcing provided by paragraph 3 and subparagraph 4(c)). In addition, even though the United States is explicitly granting U.S. citizens and residents a benefit under paragraph 5, the exception to the saving clause clarifies that under paragraph 5, the United States will not tax individuals that become U.S. citizens or residents on certain pre-emigration gain that it couldn't otherwise tax under the Convention at the time of the deemed disposition pursuant to a paragraph 5 election.

## ARTICLE 24 (NON-DISCRIMINATION)

This Article ensures that nationals of a Contracting State, in the case of paragraph 1, and residents of a Contracting State, in the case of paragraphs 2 through 5, will not be subject, directly or indirectly, to discriminatory taxation in the other Contracting State. Not all differences in tax treatment, either as between nationals of the two States, or between residents of the two States, are violations of the prohibition against discrimination. Rather, the non-discrimination obligations of this Article apply only if the nationals or residents of the two States are comparably situated.

Each of the relevant paragraphs of the Article provides that two persons that are comparably situated must be treated similarly. Although the actual words differ from paragraph to paragraph (*e.g.*, paragraph 1 refers to two nationals "in the same circumstances," paragraph 2 refers to two enterprises "carrying on the same activities," and paragraph 4 refers to two enterprises that are "similar"), the common underlying premise is that if the difference in treatment is directly related to a tax-relevant difference in the situations of the domestic and foreign persons being compared, that difference is not to be treated as discriminatory (*i.e.*, if one person is taxable in a Contracting State on worldwide income and the other is not, or tax may be collectible from one person at a later stage, but not from the other, distinctions in treatment would be justified under paragraph 1). Other examples of such factors that can lead to non-discriminatory differences in treatment are noted in the discussions of each paragraph.

The operative paragraphs of the Article also use different language to identify the kinds of differences in taxation treatment that will be considered discriminatory. For example, paragraphs 1 and 4 speak of "any taxation or any requirement connected therewith that is more burdensome," while paragraph 2 specifies that a tax "shall not be less favorably levied." Regardless of these differences in language, only differences in tax treatment that materially disadvantage the foreign person relative to the domestic person are properly the subject of the Article.

*Paragraph 1*

Paragraph 1 provides that a national of one Contracting State may not be subject to taxation or connected requirements in the other Contracting State that are more burdensome than the taxes and connected requirements imposed upon a national of that other State in the same circumstances. Since paragraph 1 prevents different treatment based on nationality, but only with respect to persons "in the same circumstances, in particular with respect to residence," it is important to distinguish, for purposes of the paragraph, a different treatment that is solely based on nationality from a different treatment that relates to other circumstances and, in particular, taxation on worldwide income.

The term "national" in relation to a Contracting State is defined in subparagraph 1(j) of Article 3 (General Definitions). The term includes both individuals and juridical persons. A national of a Contracting State is afforded protection under this paragraph even if the national is not a resident of either Contracting State. Thus, a U.S. citizen who is resident in a third country is entitled, under this paragraph, to the same treatment in Poland as a national of Poland who is in similar circumstances (*i.e.*, presumably one who is resident in a third State).

As noted above, whether or not the two persons are both taxable on worldwide income is a significant circumstance for this purpose. Accordingly, the United States is not obligated to apply the same taxing regime to a national of Poland who is not resident in the United States as it applies to a U.S. national who is not resident in the United States. U. S. citizens who are not residents of the United States but who are nevertheless subject to U. S. tax on their worldwide income are not in the same circumstances with respect to U. S. taxation as citizens of Poland who are not U. S. residents. Thus, for example, Article 24 would not entitle a national of Poland resident in a third country to taxation at graduated rates on U.S. source dividends or other invest-ment income that applies to a U.S. citizen resident in the same third country.

*Paragraph 2*

Paragraph 2 of the Article, provides that a Contracting State may not tax a permanent establishment of an enterprise of the other Contracting State less favorably than an enterprise of that first-mentioned State that is carrying on the same activities.

The fact that a U.S. permanent establishment of an enterprise of Poland is subject to U.S. tax only on income that is attributable to the permanent establishment, while a U.S. corporation engaged in the same activities is taxable on its worldwide income is not, in itself, a sufficient difference to provide different treatment for the permanent establishment. There are cases, however, where the two enterprises would not be similarly situated and differences in treatment may be warranted. For instance, it would not be a violation of the non-discrimination protection of paragraph 2 to require the foreign enterprise to provide information in a reasonable manner that may be different from the information requirements imposed on a resident enterprise, because information may not be as readily available to the Internal Revenue Service from a foreign as from a domestic enterprise. Similarly, it would not be a violation of paragraph 2 to impose penalties on persons who fail to comply with such a requirement (*see, e.g.*, sections 874(a) and 882(c)(2)). Further, a determination that income and expenses have been attributed or allocated to a permanent establishment in conformity with the principles of Article 7 (Business Profits) implies that the attribution or allocation was not discriminatory.

Section 1446 of the Code imposes the obligation to withhold tax on amounts allocable to a foreign partner on any partnership with income that is effectively connected with a U.S. trade or business. In the context of the Convention, this obligation applies with respect to a share of the partnership income of a partner resident in Poland, and attributable to a U.S. permanent establishment. There is no similar obligation with respect to the distributive shares of U.S. resident partners. It is understood, however, that this distinction is not a form of discrimination within the meaning of paragraph 2 of the Article. No distinction is made between U.S. and non-U.S. partnerships, since the law requires that partnerships of both U.S. and non-U.S. domicile withhold tax in respect of the partnership shares of non-U.S. partners. Furthermore, in distinguishing between U.S. and non-U.S. partners, the requirement to withhold on the non-U.S. but not the U.S. partner's share is not discriminatory taxation, but, like other withholding on nonresident aliens, is merely a reasonable method for the collection of tax from persons who are not continually present in the United States, and as to whom it otherwise may be difficult for the United States to enforce its tax jurisdiction. If tax has been over-withheld, the partner can, as in other cases of over-withholding, file for a refund.

*Paragraph 3*

Paragraph 3 makes clear that the provisions of paragraphs 1 and 2 do not obligate a Contracting State to grant to a resident of the other Contracting State any tax allowances, reliefs, etc., that it grants to its own residents on account of their civil status or family responsibilities. Thus, if a sole proprietor who is a resident of Poland has a permanent establishment in the United States, in assessing income tax on the profits attributable to the permanent establishment, the United States is not obligated to allow to the resident of Poland the personal allowances for himself and his family that he would be permitted to take if the permanent establishment were a sole proprietorship owned and operated by a U.S. resident, despite the fact that the individual income tax rates would apply.

*Paragraph 4*

Paragraph 4 prohibits discrimination in the allowance of deductions. When a resident or an enterprise of a Contracting State pays interest, royalties or other disbursements to a resident of the other Contracting State, the first-mentioned Contracting State must allow a deduction for those payments in computing the taxable profits of the resident or enterprise as if the payment had been made under the same conditions to a resident of the first-mentioned Contracting State. Paragraph 3, however, does not require a Contracting State to give non-residents more favorable treatment than it gives to its own residents. Consequently, a Contracting State does not have to allow non-residents a deduction for items that are not deductible under its domestic law (for example, expenses of a capital nature).

The term "other disbursements" is understood to include a reasonable allocation of executive and general administrative expenses, research and development expenses and other expenses incurred for the benefit of a group of related persons that includes the person incurring the expense.

An exception to the rule of paragraph 4 is provided for cases where the provisions of paragraph 1 of Article 9 (Associated Enterprises), paragraph 8 of Article 11 (Interest) or paragraph 6 of Article 13 (Royalties) apply. All of these provisions permit the denial of deductions in certain circumstances in respect of transactions between related persons. Neither State is forced to apply the non-discrimination principle in such cases. The exception with respect to paragraph 8 of Article 11 would include the denial or deferral of certain interest deductions under Code section 163(j).

Paragraph 4 also provides that any debts of an enterprise of a Contracting State to a resident of the other Contracting State are deductible in the first-mentioned Contracting State for purposes of computing the capital tax of the enterprise under the same conditions as if the debt had been contracted to a resident of the first-mentioned Contracting State. Even though, for general purposes, the Convention covers only income taxes, under paragraph 7 of this Article, the non-discrimination provisions apply to all taxes levied in both Contracting States, at all levels of government. Thus, this provision may be relevant for both States. The other Contracting State may have capital taxes and in the United States such taxes frequently are imposed by local governments.

*Paragraph 5*

Paragraph 5 requires that a Contracting State not impose more burdensome taxation or connected requirements on an enterprise of that State that is wholly or partly owned or controlled, directly or indirectly, by one or more residents of the other Contracting State than the taxation or connected requirements that it imposes on other similar enterprises of that first-mentioned Contracting State. For this purpose it is understood that "similar" refers to similar activities or ownership of the enterprise.

This rule, like all non-discrimination provisions, does not prohibit differing treatment of entities that are in differing circumstances. Rather, a protected enterprise is only required to be treated in the same manner as other enterprises that, from the point of view of the application of the tax law, are in substantially similar circumstances both in law and in fact. The taxation of a distributing corporation under section 367(e) on an applicable distribution to foreign shareholders does not violate paragraph 5 of the Article because a foreign-owned corporation is not similar to a domestically-owned corporation that is accorded non-recognition treatment under sections 337 and 355.

For the reasons given above in connection with the discussion of paragraph 2 of the Article, it is also understood that the provision in section 1446 of the Code for withholding of tax on non-U.S. partners does not violate paragraph 5 of the Article.

It is further understood that the ineligibility of a U.S. corporation with nonresident alien shareholders to make an election to be an "S" corporation does not violate paragraph 5 of the Article. If a corporation elects to be an S corporation, it is generally not subject to income tax and the shareholders take into account their pro rata shares of the corporation's items of income, loss, deduction or credit. A nonresident alien does not pay U.S. tax on a net basis, and, thus, does not generally take into account items of loss, deduction or credit. Therefore, the S corporation provisions do not exclude corporations with nonresident alien shareholders because such shareholders are foreign, but only because they are not net-basis taxpayers. Similarly, the provisions exclude corporations with other types of shareholders where the purpose of the provisions cannot be fulfilled or their mechanics implemented. For example, corporations with corporate shareholders are excluded because the purpose of the provision to permit individuals to conduct a business in corporate form at individual tax rates would not be furthered by their inclusion.

Finally, it is understood that paragraph 5 does not require a Contracting State to allow foreign corporations to join in filing a consolidated return with a domestic corporation or to allow similar benefits between domestic and foreign enterprises.

*Paragraph 6*

Paragraph 6 of the Article confirms that no provision of the Article will prevent either Contracting State from imposing the branch profits tax described in paragraph 1 of Article 12 (Branch Profits).

*Paragraph 7*

As noted above, notwithstanding the specification of taxes covered by the Convention in Article 2 (Taxes Covered) for general purposes, for purposes of providing nondiscrimination protection this Article applies to taxes of every kind and description imposed by a Contracting State or a political subdivision or local authority thereof. Customs duties are not considered to be taxes for this purpose.

*Relationship to Other Articles*

The saving clause of paragraph 4 of Article 1 (General Scope) does not apply to this Article by virtue of the exceptions in subparagraph 5(a) of Article 1. Thus, for example, a U.S. citizen who is a resident of the other Contracting State may claim benefits in the United States under this Article.

Nationals of a Contracting State may claim the benefits of paragraph 1 regardless of whether they are entitled to benefits under Article 22 (Limitation on Benefits), because that paragraph applies to nationals and not residents. They may not claim the benefits of the other paragraphs of this Article with respect to an item of income unless they are generally entitled to treaty benefits with respect to that income under a provision of Article 22.

## ARTICLE 25 (MUTUAL AGREEMENT PROCEDURE)

This Article provides the mechanism for taxpayers to bring to the attention of competent authorities issues and problems that may arise under the Convention. It also provides the authority for cooperation between the competent authorities of the Contracting States to resolve disputes and clarify issues that may arise under the Convention and to resolve cases of double taxation not provided for in the Convention. The competent authorities of the two Contracting States are identified in paragraph 1(g) of Article 3 (General Definitions).

*Paragraph 1*

This paragraph provides that, where a resident of a Contracting State considers that the actions of one or both Contracting States will result in taxation that is not in accordance with the Convention, he may, irrespective of the remedies provided by the domestic laws of the two Contracting States including any prescribed times limits for presenting claims for refund, present his case to the competent authority of the Contracting State of which he is a resident, or if his case comes under paragraph 1 of Article 24 (Non-Discrimination), to that of the Contracting State of which he is a national. Paragraph 1 requires that the case must be presented within three years from the first notification of the action resulting in taxation not in accordance with the provisions of the Convention.

Although the typical cases brought under this paragraph will involve economic double taxation arising from transfer pricing adjustments, the scope of this paragraph is not limited to such cases. For example, a taxpayer could request assistance from the competent authority if one Contracting State determines that the taxpayer has received deferred compensation taxable at source under Article 14 (Income from Employment), while the taxpayer believes that such income should be treated as a pension that is taxable only in his country of residence pursuant to Article 18 (Pensions, Social Security, Annuities, Alimony, and Child Support).

*Paragraph 2*

Paragraph 2 sets out the framework within which the competent authorities will deal with cases brought by taxpayers under paragraph 1. It provides that, if the competent authority of the

Contracting State to which the case is presented judges the case to have merit, and cannot reach a unilateral solution, it shall seek an agreement with the competent authority of the other Contracting State pursuant to which taxation not in accordance with the Convention will be avoided.

Any agreement is to be implemented even if such implementation otherwise would be barred by the statute of limitations or by some other procedural limitation, such as a closing agreement. Paragraph 2, however, does not prevent the application of domestic-law procedural limitations that give effect to the agreement (*e.g.*, a domestic-law requirement that the taxpayer file a return reflecting the agreement within one year of the date of the agreement).

Where the taxpayer has entered a closing agreement (or other written settlement) with the United States before bringing a case to the competent authorities, the U.S. competent authority will endeavor only to obtain a correlative adjustment from the other Contracting State. *See* Rev. Proc. 2002-52, 2002-31 I.R.B. 242, § 7.04 (or any similarly applicable or successor procedures). Because, as specified in paragraph 2 of Article 1 (General Scope), the Convention cannot operate to increase a taxpayer's liability, temporal or other procedural limitations can be overridden only for the purpose of making refunds and not to impose additional tax. Thus, even if the statute of limitations has expired, a refund of tax can be made in order to implement a correlative adjustment.

*Paragraph 3*

Paragraph 3 authorizes the competent authorities to resolve difficulties or doubts that may arise as to the application or interpretation of the Convention.

The competent authorities may, for example, agree to the same allocation of income, deductions, credits or allowances between an enterprise in one Contracting State and its permanent establishment in the other or between related persons. These allocations are to be made in accordance with the arm's length principle underlying Article 7 (Business Profits) and Article 9 (Associated Enterprises). Agreements reached under these subparagraphs may include agreement on a methodology for determining an appropriate transfer price, on an acceptable range of results under that methodology, or on a common treatment of a taxpayer's cost sharing arrangement.

The competent authorities also may agree to settle a variety of conflicting applications of the Convention. They may agree to settle conflicts regarding the characterization of particular items of income, the characterization of persons, the application of source rules to particular items of income, the meaning of a term, or the timing of an item of income.

The competent authorities may agree as to advance pricing arrangements. They also may agree as to the application of the provisions of domestic law regarding penalties, fines, and interest in a manner consistent with the purposes of the Convention.

The competent authorities may seek agreement on a uniform set of standards for the use of exchange rates. Agreements reached by the competent authorities under paragraph 3 need not conform to the internal law provisions of either Contracting State.

Paragraph 3 authorizes the competent authorities to consult for the purpose of eliminating double taxation in cases not provided for in the Convention and to resolve any difficulties or doubts arising as to the interpretation or application of the Convention. This provision is intended to permit the competent authorities to implement the treaty in particular cases in a manner that is consistent with its expressed general purposes. It permits the competent authorities to deal with cases that are within the spirit of the provisions but that are not specifically covered. An example of such a case might be double taxation arising from a transfer pricing adjustment between two permanent establishments of a third-country resident, one in the United States and one in Poland. Since no resident of a Contracting State is involved in the case, the Convention does not apply, but the competent authorities nevertheless may use the authority of this Article to prevent the double taxation of income.

*Paragraph 4*

Paragraph 4 provides that the competent authorities may communicate with each other for the purpose of reaching an agreement. This makes clear that the competent authorities of the two Contracting States may communicate without going through diplomatic channels. Such communication may be in various forms, including, where appropriate, through a joint commission consisting of themselves or their representatives.

*Treaty termination in relation to competent authority dispute resolution*

A case may be raised by a taxpayer under a treaty with respect to a year for which a treaty was in force after the treaty has been terminated. In such a case the ability of the competent authorities to act is limited. They may not exchange confidential information, nor may they reach a solution that varies from that specified in its law.

*Triangular competent authority solutions*

International tax cases may involve more than two taxing jurisdictions (*e.g.*, transactions among a parent corporation resident in country A and its subsidiaries resident in countries B and C). As long as there is a complete network of treaties among the three countries, it should be possible, under the full combination of bilateral authorities, for the competent authorities of the three States to work together on a three-sided solution. Although country A may not be able to give information received under Article 26 (Exchange of Information) from country B to the authorities of country C, if the competent authorities of the three countries are working together, it should not be a problem for them to arrange for the authorities of country B to give the necessary information directly to the tax authorities of country C, as well as to those of country A. Each bilateral part of the trilateral solution must, of course, not exceed the scope of the authority of the competent authorities under the relevant bilateral treaty.

*Relationship to Other Articles*

This Article is not subject to the saving clause of paragraph 4 of Article 1 (General

91

Scope) by virtue of the exceptions in paragraph 5(a) of that Article. Thus, rules, definitions, procedures, etc. that are agreed upon by the competent authorities under this Article may be applied by the United States with respect to its citizens and residents even if they differ from the comparable Code provisions. Similarly, as indicated above, U.S. law may be overridden to provide refunds of tax to a U.S. citizen or resident under this Article. A person may seek relief under this Article regardless of whether he is generally entitled to benefits under Article 22 (Limitation on Benefits). As in all other cases, the competent authority is vested with the discretion to decide whether the claim for relief is justified.

## ARTICLE 26 (EXCHANGE OF INFORMATION)

This Article provides for the exchange of information and administrative assistance between the competent authorities of the Contracting States. While mutual agreement procedures are addressed in Article 25 (Mutual Agreement Procedure), exchanges of information for purposes of the mutual agreement procedures are governed by this Article.

*Paragraph 1*

The obligation to obtain and provide information to the other Contracting State is set out in Paragraph 1. The information to be exchanged is that which is foreseeably relevant for carrying out the provisions of the Convention or the domestic laws of the United States or Poland concerning taxes of every kind applied at the national level. This language incorporates the standard of the OECD Model. The Contracting States intend for the phrase "is foreseeably relevant" to be interpreted to permit the exchange of information that "may be relevant" for purposes of Section 7602 of the Code, which authorizes the IRS to examine "any books, papers, records, or other data which *may* be relevant or material" (emphasis added). In United States v. Arthur Young & Co., 465 U.S. 805, 814 (1984), the Supreme Court stated that the language "may be" reflects Congress's express intention to allow the IRS to obtain "items of even *potential* relevance to an ongoing investigation, without reference to its admissibility" (emphasis in original.) However, the language "may be" would not support a request in which a Contracting State simply asked for information regarding all bank accounts maintained by residents of that Contracting State in the other Contracting State. Thus, the language of paragraph 1 is intended to provide for exchange of information in tax matters to the widest extent possible, while clarifying that Contracting States are not at liberty to engage in "fishing expeditions" or otherwise to request information that is unlikely to be relevant to the tax affairs of a given taxpayer.

Consistent with the OECD Model, a request for information does not constitute a "fishing expedition" solely because it does not provide the name or address (or both) of the taxpayer under examination or investigation. In cases where the requesting State does not provide the name or address (or both) of the taxpayer under examination or investigation, the requesting State must provide other information sufficient to identify the taxpayer. Similarly, paragraph 1 does not necessarily require the request to include the name and/or address of the person believed to be in possession of the information.

The standard of "foreseeable relevance" can be met in cases dealing with both one taxpayer (whether identified by name or otherwise) or several taxpayers (whether identified by name or otherwise). Where a Contracting State undertakes an investigation into an ascertainable group or category of persons in accordance with its laws, any request related to the investigation will typically serve the objective of carrying out the domestic tax laws of the requesting State and thus will comply with the requirements of paragraph 1, provided it meets the standard of "foreseeable relevance." In such cases, the requesting State should provide, supported by a clear factual basis, a detailed description of the group or category of persons and of the specific facts and circumstances that have led to the request, as well as an explanation of the applicable law and why there is reason to believe that the taxpayers in the group or category of persons for whom information is requested have been non-compliant with that law. The requesting State should further show that the requested information would assist in determining compliance by the taxpayers in the group or category of persons.

Exchange of information with respect to each State's domestic law is authorized to the extent that taxation under domestic law is not contrary to the Convention. Thus, for example, information may be exchanged under this Article even if the transaction to which the information relates is a purely domestic transaction in the requesting State and, therefore, the exchange is not made to carry out the Convention. An example of such a case is provided in subparagraph 8(b) of the OECD Commentary: a company resident in one Contracting State and a company resident in the other Contracting State transact business between themselves through a third-country resident company. Neither Contracting State has a treaty with the third state. To enforce their internal laws with respect to transactions of their residents with the third-country company (since there is no relevant treaty in force), the Contracting States may exchange information regarding the prices that their residents paid in their transactions with the third-country resident.

Paragraph 1 clarifies that information may be exchanged that relates to the assessment or collection of, the enforcement or prosecution in respect of, or the determination of appeals in relation to, taxes of every kind imposed by a Contracting State at the national level. Accordingly, the competent authorities may request and provide information for cases under examination or criminal investigation, in collection, on appeals, or under prosecution, and information may be exchanged with respect to U.S. estate and gift taxes.

Information exchange is not restricted by paragraph 1 of Article 1 (General Scope). Accordingly, information may be requested and provided under this Article with respect to persons who are not residents of either Contracting State. For example, if a third-country resident has a permanent establishment in the other Contracting State, and that permanent establishment engages in transactions with a U.S. enterprise, the United States could request information with respect to that permanent establishment, even though the third-country resident is not a resident of either Contracting State. Similarly, if a third-country resident maintains a bank account in the other Contracting State, and the Internal Revenue Service has reason to believe that funds in that account should have been reported for U.S. tax purposes but have not been so reported, information can be requested from the other Contracting State with respect to that person's account, even though that person is not the taxpayer under examination.

Although the term "United States" does not encompass U.S. possessions or territories for most purposes of the Convention, section 7651 of the Code authorizes the Internal Revenue

Service to utilize the administrative and enforcement provisions of the Code in the U.S. possessions or territories, including to obtain information pursuant to a proper request made under Article 26. If necessary to obtain requested information, the Internal Revenue Service could issue and enforce an administrative summons to the taxpayer, a tax authority (or other U.S. possession or territory government agency), or a third party located in a U.S. possession or territory.

*Paragraph 2*

Paragraph 2 provides assurances that any information exchanged will be treated as secret, subject to the same disclosure constraints as information obtained under the laws of the requesting State. The confidentiality rules cover communications between the competent authorities (including the letter requesting information) as well as references to exchanged information that may occur in other documents, such as advice by government attorneys to their respective competent authorities. At the same time, it is understood that the requested State can disclose the minimum information contained in a competent authority letter (but not the letter itself) necessary for the requested State to be able to obtain or provide the requested information to the requesting State, without frustrating the efforts of the requesting State. If, however, court proceedings or the like under the domestic laws of the requested State necessitate the disclosure of the competent authority letter itself, the competent authority of the requested State may disclose such a letter unless the requesting State otherwise specifies.

Information received may be disclosed only to persons or authorities, including courts and administrative bodies, involved in the assessment, collection, or administration of, the enforcement or prosecution in respect of, or the determination of appeals in relation to, the taxes referred to in paragraph 1. Under this standard, information may be communicated to the taxpayer or his proxy. The information must be used by these persons only for the purposes mentioned in paragraph 2. Information may also be disclosed to legislative bodies, such as the tax-writing committees of the U.S. Congress and the U.S. Government Accountability Office, engaged in the oversight of the preceding activities. Information received by these bodies must be for use in the performance of their role in overseeing the administration of U.S. tax laws. Information received may be disclosed in public court proceedings or in judicial decisions.

In situations in which the requested State determines that the requesting State does not comply with its duties regarding the confidentiality of the information exchanged under this Article, the requested State may suspend assistance under this Article until such time as proper assurance is given by the requesting State that those duties will indeed be respected. If necessary, the competent authorities may enter into specific arrangements or memoranda of understanding regarding the confidentiality of the information exchanged under this Article.

*Paragraph 3*

Paragraph 3 provides that the obligations undertaken in paragraphs 1 and 2 to exchange information do not require a Contracting State to carry out administrative measures that are at variance with the laws or administrative practice of either State. Nor is a Contracting State required to supply information not obtainable under the laws or administrative practice of either State, or to disclose trade secrets or other information, the disclosure of which would be contrary to public policy.

Thus, a requesting State may be denied information from the other State if the information would be obtained pursuant to procedures or measures that are broader than those available in the requesting State. However, the statute of limitations of the Contracting State making the request for information should govern a request for information. Thus, the Contracting State of which the request is made should attempt to obtain the information even if its own statute of limitations has passed. In many cases, relevant information will still exist in the business records of the taxpayer or a third party, even though it is no longer required to be kept for domestic tax purposes.

While paragraph 3 states conditions under which a Contracting State is not obligated to comply with a request from the other Contracting State for information, the requested State is not precluded from providing such information, and may, at its discretion, do so subject to the limitations of its internal law.

*Paragraph 4*

Paragraph 4 provides that when information is requested by a Contracting State in accordance with this Article, the other Contracting State is obligated to obtain the requested information as if the tax in question were the tax of the requested State, even if that State has no direct tax interest in the case to which the request relates. In the absence of such a paragraph, some taxpayers have argued that paragraph 3(a) prevents a Contracting State from requesting information from a bank or fiduciary that the Contracting State does not need for its own tax purposes. This paragraph clarifies that paragraph 3 does not impose such a restriction and that a Contracting State is not limited to providing only the information that it already has in its own files.

*Paragraph 5*

Paragraph 5 provides that a Contracting State may not decline to provide information because that information is held by banks, other financial institutions, nominees or persons acting in an agency or fiduciary capacity or because it relates to ownership interests in a person. Thus, paragraph 5 would effectively prevent a Contracting State from relying on paragraph 3 to argue that its domestic bank secrecy laws (or similar legislation relating to disclosure of financial information by financial institutions or intermediaries) override its obligation to provide information under paragraph 1. This paragraph also requires the disclosure of information regarding the beneficial owner of an interest in a person, such as the identity of a beneficial owner of bearer shares.

Subparagraphs (3)(a) and (b) do not permit the requested State to decline a request where paragraph 4 or 5 applies. Paragraph 5 would apply, for instance, in situations in which the requested State's inability to obtain the information was specifically related to the fact that the requested information was believed to be held by a bank or other financial institution. Thus, the application of paragraph 5 includes situations in which the tax authorities' information gathering powers with respect to information held by banks and other financial institutions are subject to different requirements than those that are generally applicable with respect to information held by persons other than banks or other financial institutions. This would, for example, be the case where the tax authorities can only exercise their information gathering powers with respect to information held by banks and other financial institutions in instances where specific information on the taxpayer under examination or investigation is available. This would also be the case where, for example, the use of information gathering measures with respect to information held by banks and other financial institutions requires a higher probability that the information requested is held by the person believed to be in possession of the requested information than the degree of probability required for the use of information gathering measures with respect to information believed to be held by persons other than banks or financial institutions.

*Paragraph 6*

Paragraph 6 provides that the requesting State may specify the form in which information is to be provided (*e.g.*, depositions of witnesses and authenticated copies of original documents). The intention is to ensure that the information may be introduced as evidence in the judicial proceedings of the requesting State. The requested State should, if possible, provide the information in the form requested to the same extent that it can obtain information in that form under its own laws and administrative practices with respect to its own taxes.

*Paragraph 7*

Paragraph 7 states that the competent authorities of the Contracting States may develop an agreement upon the mode of application of the Article. The Article authorizes the competent authorities to exchange information on an automatic basis, on request in relation to a specific case, or spontaneously. It is contemplated that the Contracting States will utilize this authority to engage in all of these forms of information exchange, as appropriate.

The competent authorities may also agree on specific procedures and timetables for the exchange of information. In particular, the competent authorities may agree on minimum thresholds regarding tax at stake or take other measures aimed at ensuring some measure of reciprocity with respect to the overall exchange of information between the Contracting States.

*Treaty effective dates and termination in relation to exchange of information*

Once the Convention is in force, the competent authority may seek information under the Convention with respect to a year prior to the entry into force of the Convention. Even if an earlier Convention with more restrictive provisions, or even no Convention, was in effect during the years in which the transaction at issue occurred, the exchange of information provisions of the Convention apply. In that case, the competent authorities have available to them the full range of information exchange provisions afforded under this Article.

In contrast, if the Convention is terminated in accordance with the provisions of Article 29 (Termination), it would cease to authorize, as of the date of termination, any exchange of information, even with respect to a year for which the Convention was in force. In such case, the tax administrations of the two countries would only be able to exchange information to the extent allowed under either domestic law or another international agreement or arrangement.

## ARTICLE 27 (MEMBERS OF DIPLOMATIC MISSIONS AND CONSULAR POSTS)

This Article confirms that any fiscal privileges to which diplomatic or consular officials are entitled under general provisions of international law or under special agreements will apply notwithstanding any provisions to the contrary in the Convention. The agreements referred to include any bilateral agreements, such as consular conventions, that affect the taxation of diplomats and consular officials and any multilateral agreements dealing with these issues, such as the Vienna Convention on Diplomatic Relations and the Vienna Convention on Consular Relations. The U.S. generally adheres to the latter because its terms are consistent with customary international law.

The Article does not independently provide any benefits to diplomatic agents and consular officers. Article 19 (Government Service) does so, as do Code section 893 and a number of bilateral and multilateral agreements. In the event that there is a conflict between the Convention and international law or such other treaties, under which the diplomatic agent or consular official is entitled to greater benefits under the latter, the latter laws or agreements shall have precedence. Conversely, if the Convention confers a greater benefit than another agreement, the affected person could claim the benefit of the tax treaty.

Pursuant to subparagraph 5(b) of Article 1, the saving clause of paragraph 4 of Article 1 (General Scope) does not apply to override any benefits of this Article available to an individual who is neither a citizen of the United States nor has immigrant status in the United States.

## ARTICLE 28 (ENTRY INTO FORCE)

This Article contains the rules for bringing the Convention into force and giving effect to its provisions.

*Paragraph 1*

Paragraph 1 provides for the ratification of the Convention by both Contracting States according to their constitutional and statutory requirements. This paragraph requires the Contracting States to notify each other in writing, through diplomatic channel, when their respective applicable procedures have been satisfied.

In the United States, the process leading to ratification and entry into force is as follows: Once a treaty has been signed by authorized representatives of the two Contracting States, the Department of State sends the treaty to the President who formally transmits it to the Senate for its advice and consent to ratification, which requires approval by two-thirds of the Senators present and voting. Prior to this vote, however, it generally has been the practice for the Senate Committee on Foreign Relations to hold hearings on the treaty and make a recommendation regarding its approval to the full Senate. Both Government and private sector witnesses may testify at these hearings. After the Senate gives its advice and consent to ratification of the protocol or treaty, an instrument of ratification is drafted for the President's signature. The President's signature completes the process in the United States.

*Paragraph 2*

Paragraph 2 provides that the Convention will enter into force on the date of the later of the diplomatic notes referred to in paragraph 1. The date on which a treaty enters into force is not necessarily the date on which its provisions take effect. Paragraph 2, therefore, also contains rules that determine when the provisions of the treaty will have effect.

Under subparagraph 2(a), the Convention will have effect with respect to taxes withheld at source (principally dividends, interest and royalties) for amounts paid or credited on or after the first day of the second month following the date on which the Convention enters into force. For example, if instruments of ratification are exchanged on April 25 of a given year, the withholding rates specified in paragraph 2 of Article 10 (Dividends) would be applicable to any dividends paid or credited on or after June 1 of that year. This rule allows the benefits of the withholding reductions to be put into effect as soon as possible, without waiting until the following year. The delay of one to two months is required to allow sufficient time for withholding agents to be informed about the change in withholding rates. If for some reason a withholding agent withholds at a higher rate than that provided by the Convention (perhaps because it was not able to re-program its computers before the payment is made), a beneficial owner of the income that is a resident of the other Contracting State may make a claim for refund pursuant to section 1464 of the Code.

For all other taxes, subparagraph 2(b) specifies that the Convention will have effect for any taxable period beginning on or after January 1 of the year following entry into force.

*Paragraph 3*

Paragraph 3 provides that the Convention between the Government of the United States of America and the Government of the Polish People's Republic for the Avoidance of Double Taxation and the Prevention of Fiscal Evasion with Respect to Taxes on Income signed at Washington on October 8, 1974 (hereinafter referred to as "the 1974 convention") shall cease to have effect in relation to any tax from the date upon which this Convention has effect in respect of such tax in accordance with the provisions of paragraph 2 of this Article. The 1974 convention shall terminate on the last date on which it has effect in relation to any tax in accordance with the foregoing provisions of this paragraph.

*Paragraph 4*

Paragraph 4 provides that notwithstanding the entry into force of this Convention, an individual who was entitled to benefits of Article 17 (Teachers), Article 18 (Students and Trainees) or Article 19 (Government Functions) of the 1974 convention at the time of the entry into force of this Convention shall continue to be entitled to such benefits until such time as the individual would cease to be entitled to such benefits if the 1974 convention remained in force.

## ARTICLE 29 (TERMINATION)

The Convention is to remain in effect indefinitely, unless terminated by one of the Contracting States in accordance with the provisions of Article 29. The Convention may be terminated at any time after the year in which the Convention enters into force. The Article requires that any notices of termination must be given through diplomatic channels, and must be delivered on or before June 30 in any calendar beginning after the year in which the Convention enters into force. If such notice of termination is given, the provisions of the Convention with respect to withholding at source will cease to have effect on or after the first day of January of the calendar year next following the date on which the notice has been given. For other taxes, the Convention will cease to have effect as of taxable periods beginning on or after the first day of January of the calendar year next following the date on which the notice is given.

Article 29 relates only to unilateral termination of the Convention by a Contracting State. Nothing in that Article should be construed as preventing the Contracting States from concluding a new bilateral agreement, subject to ratification, that supersedes, amends or terminates provisions of the Convention without the six-month notification period.

Customary international law observed by the United States and other countries, as reflected in the Vienna Convention on Treaties, allows termination by one Contracting State at any time in the event of a "material breach" of the agreement by the other Contracting State.